Christianity in the Netherlands
Masterpieces from the Museum Catharijneconvent

Christianity in the Netherlands

Masterpieces from the Museum Catharijneconvent

museum Catharijneconvent | Waanders Uitgevers

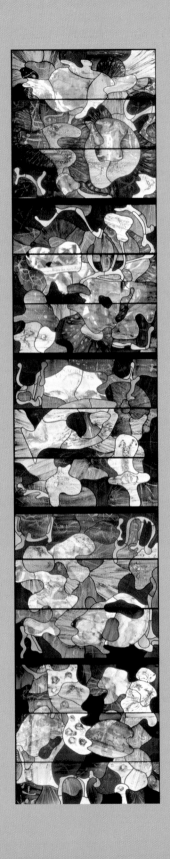

Table of contents

Foreword

The collection of the Museum Catharijneconvent is rich and diverse. Taking as its overarching theme the Christian art and culture of the Netherlands, the museum attempts to bring the fascinating history of Christianity in the Netherlands to life within the magnificent walls of a medieval cluster of buildings in the heart of Utrecht.

The museum first opened its doors to the public in 1979. Around the year 2000 it became increasingly apparent the time had come to restore the buildings and to revitalise the badly dated permanent display. In the process of achieving this, key exhibits in the permanent collection were removed from view for several years. Now, after four years of hard work, the museum's permanent display has been completed and the collection's highlights glitter in renewed glory within the restored museum walls.

The broad basis of the Museum Catharijneconvent's collection comprises the collections of the Aartsbisschoppelijk Museum in Utrecht, Haarlem's Bisschoppelijk Museum, the Oud-katholiek Museum and the Stichting Protestants Kerkelijk Kunstbezit. Acting on the initiative of central government, the four placed their collections with the Stichting Catharijneconvent. Not only could the collections be better managed in this way, but their amalgamation led also – almost inadvertently – to the creation of one of the most important museums of Christian art and culture in the world. An important additional factor was that, remarkably, the various collections transpired to fit seamlessly with one another, thereby further strengthening the fledgling museum's offering. The Aartsbisschoppelijk Museum, for example, owns a magnificent collection of medieval art while the three other collections are outstanding in the period after 1600. The collections have been further enriched with a selection of loans from the Diocesan Museums of Breda, 's Hertogenbosch and Roermond. In addition the museum can draw on the state collections, while a number of private individuals have been willing to give works on long loan. A policy of careful purchases is aimed at closing any gaps in the collections and forging a lasting unity within the whole. In this regard we cannot fail to mention the extremely generous support of the Association of Friends of the Museum Catharijneconvent. Thanks to their efforts, many an ostensibly unattainable object has gained a place within the museum.

The works of art shown and described here have been carefully selected for their artistic significance, their role within the history of Christianity in the Netherlands and their art historical relevance. The context significantly bolsters their artistic worth. For the first time in its history, the Museum Catharijneconvent affords a permanent consideration of the recent history of Christian culture. In the future, the museum aims to make a contribution towards the development of Christian art in the Netherlands. It is important, therefore, that we gain an accurate picture of the period after 1945. In recent years we have formulated and implemented policy to this end. This is reflected, among other things, in the fact that all the works of art described in the final chapter have been acquired recently and/or have not previously been on display in the museum.

To mark the occasion of the re-opening of the museum, a monumental stained glass window by the artist Marc Mulders will be mounted in the central stairwell. The theme chosen is the 'Apocalypse' (ill. p. 4). We specifically chose Marc Mulders for this commission because he is an outstanding example of someone who works within the Christian tradition but at the same time revitalises it in inspiring and innovative ways.

I am exceedingly grateful to the various authors for their contributions to this book. They have acquitted themselves magnificently of their task. The collection has been viewed with new eyes. And that is a good thing: each generation should study the rich collections of this museum from a new viewpoint and should place new accents. That is what keeps the museum alive and its public eternally involved.

Guus van den Hout
General director

Introduction

Saskia van Haaren

The story of Christianity in the Netherlands is one of ideals, confrontation and conflict. How did people in the Netherlands believe and how do they worship today? How did the Netherlands become as it is today, what influences did the Christian religion have on Dutch society, where does our much-praised tradition of tolerance originate from and what do we actually mean when we label something as 'Calvinist'? In historical terms, what is so special about Catholicism, Protestantism and the many offshoots within the main religious movements in the Netherlands? These questions, often asked, form the point of departure for the Museum Catharijneconvent's renewed permanent display. Those who wander through the old cloister passageways will gain an overview of the history of Christianity in the Netherlands. The Museum shows the extent to which this religion has been instrumental in determining our way of thinking and living. Christianity has stamped an indelible mark on our culture. Our history is dated from the year of Christ's birth, for example, while Christian festivals such as Christmas, Easter and Whitsun all play a role in the arrangement of our year.

Through paintings, images and liturgical objects, a continuing story is told of Christianity's arrival on these shores, the spread of

360° photo of Museum Catharijneconvent taken from the cloistergarden

the faith, the role of the church in the Middle Ages and of prominent figures such as Luther and Calvin. The story continues with the multitude of religious sects in the seventeenth century, as well as the typically Dutch phenomenon of 'verzuiling' or religious compartmentalisation of social structures. The present day also figures in the story, but not as a conclusion, for the question of what Christianity means to the Netherlands remains current.

Seven themes make up the backbone of this story, both in this book as in the museum's presentation of the collection. Each era is typified by objects characteristic of the given period. In some cases these will be major works of art of particular beauty and with a unique art historical significance, at other times simple implements for domestic use. What they have in common is that each has something to say about the Netherlands. Each theme deals with important events that have influenced the way in which faith is practised in this country. The impact of such events on the present day is also examined. The museum sheds light on why particular debates with regard to the Christian religion are still being waged today and why they are so characteristic of the national identity.

The definitive account of Christianity obviously doesn't exist. Instead we have attempted to present the various eras within a coherent framework, selecting the most beautiful or most striking objects from the collection to serve as illustration. While it is impossible to offer an exhaustive account, we have attempted to do justice to the relevant aspects of the story of Christianity in the Netherlands.

In selecting the pieces to be displayed, we drew on the museum's extensive collection, which currently numbers some 60,000 objects. Paintings, sculptures, ecclesiastical garments, gold and silver liturgical implements, costly medieval illuminated manuscripts and a large range of devotionalia show the rich culture of Christianity in the Netherlands down the centuries. In particular the museum's collection of medieval art, the country's largest, is internationally well-known and reflects the influence of the church on daily life at that time. A large number of top exhibits have been included in this book. Taken together they illustrate the colourful history of Christianity in the Netherlands.

The Museum Catharijneconvent in Utrecht opened its doors to the public in 1979. The museum is housed in the attractive restored buildings of the former monastery where the Knights of the Order of St John ran a hospital in the sixteenth century. Another part of the museum is housed in a canal house linked to the former monastery via an underground tunnel. The Church of St Catherine flanking the complex was completed in the early sixteenth century. Since 1853 it has been the seat of the Roman Catholic Archbishop of Utrecht.

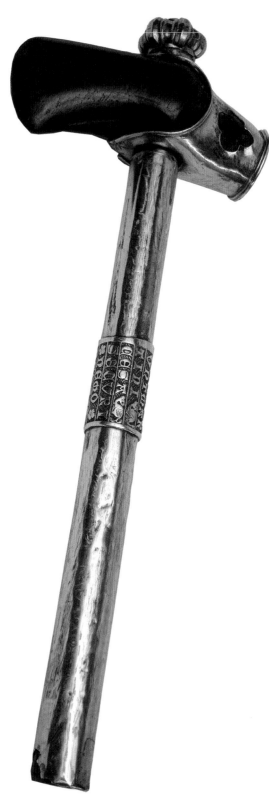

1

Hammer belonging to
St Martin, stone, around 1000
BC; handle Lower Rhine region,
around 1300 AD

According to medieval legend,
St Martin used this prehistoric
stone axe to destroy the graven
images of the heathen. For this
reason the Church of St Martin
in Utrecht preserved the axe
head carefully and around 1300
commissioned a silver handle to
be fashioned for it, bearing the
following inscription: 'The
graven images plunge to the
earth, struck by St Martin's axe.
Let no one think that those who
so easily fall can be gods'
(translated from the Latin).

1

Missionaries on the March

Janneke Raaijmakers

In the early Middle Ages the Netherlands as we know it now did not yet exist. In the tidal region along the North Sea coast the Frisians built their dwellings on mounds or 'terpen', living 'almost like fish in the waters [...] by which they are almost everywhere surrounded, with but a few exits to the outside world, unless they allow themselves to be transported by boat,' according to an 8th century historian.

The land of the Frisians was not a clearly defined political entity but a conglomerate of 'tribes' who were known collectively as Frisians. Sometimes their influence reached far into the southern Netherlands, but there were also periods in which the Franks – whose territory comprised a large part of current-day France, Belgium and the Moselle region – beat them back north of the Rhine. Unlike the Franks, the Frisians were not Christian. Little is known of their religion, but what we do know is that they believed in several gods (including Donar, Wodan, Saxnot and Fosite) and that they had their own sacred sites.

Missionaries from the Frankish kingdom such as Wulfram, bishop of Sens (†circa 700) attempted to convert the Frisian pagans to Christianity. But the best known missionaries proselytising in the land of the Frisians came from Anglo-Saxon England. Probably the most famous is Boniface due to his violent martyrdom at Dokkum in 754, but it is Willibrord (circa. 658-739) who played the most significant role in the mission to the Netherlands (ill. 2).

Willibrord was inspired by the Irish tradition of *peregrinatio pro Deo*: an extreme form of asceticism whose adherents eschewed all worldly goods in order to surrender themselves completely to God. He first set foot on Frisian soil in 690, but many had already gone before him: the Germanic territories north of the Rhine were particularly popular among missionaries because Christianity had hardly taken hold. In addition the Anglo-Saxons felt a certain affinity with these Germanic peoples. As the English historian the Venerable Bede (672/3-735) wrote: 'many tribes lived in Germania, from whom the Angles and Saxons now living in Britannia are descended.' An additional advantage of these 'communal' origins was that the missionaries in the land of the Frisians could make themselves understood. The difference between Old Frisian and Old English was in fact not very great.

Before he settled in the watery region of the Frisians, Willibrord went to the Frankish mayor of the palace Pepin II (640/650-714). At that time Pepin ranked as the king's highest official in the kingdom of the Franks. Pepin gave the monk permission to work as a missionary in the area between the Scheldt and Rhine rivers, a region that fell under his control and where he could offer Willibrord the necessary protection. Pepin, too, stood to profit from the co-operation with Willibrord. Not only did Pepin want to spread Christianity out of a sense of personal conviction, but the spread of Christianity was also a way of forging unity in the area under his control.

Willibrord ensured that he not only enjoyed the support of the worldly ruler, but also that of the most important spiritual leader in Europe, the pope. According to the eighth-century biography of Willibrord, Pope Sergius received the missionary with open arms. The Pope gave Willibrord relics of saints that the missionary could use to consecrate the altars of the churches he was to found. Relics are the remains (from the Latin *reliquiae*) of a saint. In late Antiquity and the early Middle Ages such relics were frequently 'contact' relics: objects which the saint had touched during life or in death such as a comb, for example, or a scrap of cloth from a garment. One such relic is the alb of Odulphus (ill. 3).

2

Shield for cope depicting the ordination of Willibrord, Utrecht 1505-1514

David of Burgundy, bishop of Utrecht between 1456 and 1496, commissioned the cope on which this shield is embroidered. The scene from the life of Willibrord is embroidered in gold and satin thread on cloth of velvet.

3

Fragment of the alb belonging to Odulphus, eighth-ninth century

This fragment of cloth from Odulphus' vestment is perhaps not of one the museum's most beautiful textile fragments, but in view of its age and its sacred significance it is one of the most special. Odulphus, a missionary who worked in Friesland, and who died after 854, is said to have worn this garment. Because he was a saint Odulphus' relics, including this alb, were among the most precious treasures of Utrecht's St Salvator or Oudmunster Church.

4

Merovingian reliquary, Eastern France?, around 700

Little is known about this fine gilded copper reliquary. Its ornately decorated exterior indicates that the contents it held were precious. It probably used to hang from a chain or belt, for traces of where fastenings would have been fixed are still to be seen on its sides. A farmer fished the reliquary out of the Waal River in the mid-nineteenth century.

From the eighth century, but particularly from the ninth century onwards, it became common to divide the body of the saint up into relics. Even before this period the church had been unable to prevent saints' graves from being plundered by dealers in relics or believers in search of a new patron saint. But even so the Roman regulation, that graves should on no account be disturbed in order to vouchsafe the eternal rest of the dead, still held sway. The holy treasures were often kept in beautifully decorated reliquaries which functioned both as protection and as an indication to the viewer of the high value of the contents they held. A fine example is the Merovingian reliquary dating from around 700 (ill. 4).

Because of their modest dimensions, diminutive shrines such as these were easy to transport. It is probable that missionaries such as Willibrord carried comparable reliquaries with them on their travels.

When Willibrord arrived in Utrecht he discovered – on the spot where the Dom now stands – the remains of an old church that the Frankish King Dagobert (603-639) had ordered to be built for his soldiers around the year 630. Willibrord rebuilt the church and dedicated it to Saint Martin, patron saint of the Franks. To this day Saint Martin is still Utrecht's patron saint. In addition Willibrord built the Salvator church and a monastery to school clergy able to help him in his work and carry on his mission after his death.

St Martin's hammer (ill.1, p.10) was one of the treasures of the later St Martin's Church. People believed that Martin of Tours (St Martin) had used this axe to lay waste to pagan temples and chop down pagan trees.

Working from Utrecht, Willibrord was able to carry out his missionary work unhindered for a number of years, but in 714 the Frisian leader Radbod came into conflict with the sons of Pepin II, who had died earlier that year. As a consequence Willibrord and his followers were forced to flee Utrecht. They were only able to return in 719, after the new Frankish ruler Charles Martel re-imposed his authority following Radbod's death.

5
Lebuinus' chalice, Palace School
at Aachen, early ninth century;
holder fourteenth century
It is thought that craftsmen
from Aachen fashioned this
unusual chalice, for the
acanthus patterning on the
cup strongly resembles the
decoration on the balustrade of
Charlemagne's palts (palace)
chapel in Aachen. This
Carolingian emperor was
inspired by Christian Roman
emperors such as Constantine
the Great in his attempts to
forge a single Christian empire.
The courtly interest in the late
classical period was also
reflected in the art of the time.

Most of the early missionaries working in Frisia were recruited from Anglo-Saxon areas of England. One of them, Liafwin, known as Lebuin, led missionaries from the Utrecht diocese in proselytising in Overijssel around 765. Lebuin built a chapel in Wilp, and later a church in Deventer. The precious ivory Lebuinus chalice (ill. 5) dates from the beginning of the ninth century. Contrary to traditional claims, then, it could not have been used by Lebuin himself.

Nor was the Lebuinus codex (ills. 6, 7) – despite what its name would seem to indicate - ever owned by the Anglo-Saxon missionary. Lebuin (†777) had been dead some seventy years by the time this book was finished. But while the chalice and evangelary both post-date Lebuin, they are objects that belonged in a missionary's equipment – albeit in less ornately decorated form. Lebuin would undoubtedly have carried an evangelary with him during his missionary work. In the early Middle Ages codices seldom comprised all the books of the Bible, as is common today. Quite often the four Gospels would be bound together, as happened with the Lebuinus codex. For someone on the road this was enough. Obviously the libraries of major religious communities and churches did own all the biblical texts. These were not collected in complete Bibles, but existed as separate sections.

It is unclear how the Lebuinus codex ended up in Deventer. Perhaps the church in Deventer commissioned the Utrecht scriptorium to make the book or possibly it was a showpiece belonging to the Utrecht church that was later brought to Deventer, for example in 880, when the Normans attacked towns such as Nijmegen and Maastricht. The bishop of Utrecht sought refuge in Deventer, because Frankish authority was more firmly established here. The Utrecht bishops were to remain in Deventer until around 920. It is possible that the codex could have been transferred to Deventer at that particular juncture.

Showpieces such as the Lebuinus codex were only taken out on feast days and displayed to the faithful on the altar and during processions. The chalice was used in the celebration of Mass.

As time went by the efforts of the missionaries Willibrord, Boniface and Lebuinus began to bear fruit. Christianity gained a firm foothold in the lands held by the Frisians. In 777 Utrecht became a diocese of

Saint Martin

Saint Martin († November 11, 397), born in Hungary, was an officer in the Roman army with a promising career ahead of him. According to his biographer, Sulpicious Severus, he came upon a naked beggar before the gates of Amiens one cold winter's day. Taking pity on the freezing man Martin slashed his cloak in two with his sword and gave half to the beggar. That same night Christ appeared to him in a dream. Martin consequently became baptised and several years later he left the army to lead a secluded life as a monk. But his seclusion did not last long; around 371 the people of Tours chose him as their bishop.

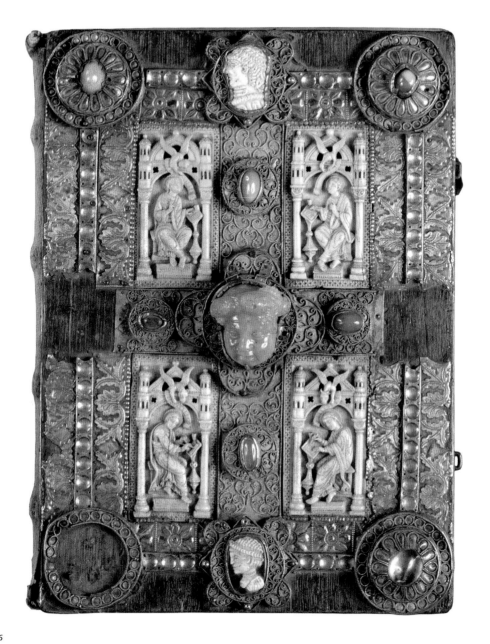

Lebuinus codex, Northern France, mid ninth century; binding Cologne, eleventh-twelfth century

The Lebuinus codex contains the four Gospels and is beautifully illuminated. It is thought that the makers of the book were members of a monastery in Northern France, for example that of the St Bertins at Saint-Omer or of the St Vaas at Atrecht (now known as Arras). The parchment manuscript was made around the middle of the ninth century. The book's covers date from the twelfth century, and have been decorated using both old (antique) and 'new' (twelfth century) materials. The cover has been extremely beautifully decorated using silver, ivory and precious stones. The four evangelists – Matthew, Mark, Luke and John, identified respectively by the winged figure, lion, ox and eagle – have been carved in walrus tusk (1150-1175). In the centre of the cross the makers have mounted a Bacchus head from antiquity (first-third century AD) from Asia Minor, with above and below it two pseudo-cameos dating from the sixth and seventh century AD.

7

Lebuinus codex, beginning of the Gospel of St Luke, Northern France, mid ninth century

The style in which the Lebuinus codex is illuminated is known as the Franco-Saxon style. This style, strongly influenced by the insular tradition (that is, deriving from Anglo-Saxon Britain and Ireland) of manuscript illumination, is characterised by its weaving patterns and plant and animal motifs. The opening words are rendered in capitals, the body text in Carolingian minuscule, a clear and regular script that came into use across Western Europe in the ninth century and continued to be used into the thirteenth century. The text shown here is that of the opening lines of the Gospel according to St Luke and reads as follows: Incipit textus eiusdem. Quoniam quidem multi conati sunt ordinare narrationem quae in nobis completae sunt rerum sicut tradiderunt nobis qui ab initio ips uideruntet ministri fuerunt sermonis etcetera. (Here begins his text. Many have since taken upon themselves to write an account of the events which took place in our midst and those which have been passed on to us by those who have been witnesses from the beginning and have become servants of the Word etcetera.'

Utrecht, which eventually was to include almost the entire area of the present-day Netherlands north of the rivers Meuse and Scheldt as well as the province of Zeeland. By now it was not only outsiders who were spreading the word but also members of local families, such as the Frisian Liudger (around 742-809). It is unclear whether the Norman invasions, particularly frequent in the period 837 to 885, had severely disrupted the conversion to Christianity of the Netherlands. The majority of sources dealing with this subject are of a later date. The conversion to Christianity was in any case a long drawn-out process. For a considerable period of time various religious traditions and pagan rites continued to exist alongside one another.

In the early tenth century Utrecht became part of the eastern Frankish Empire, where the Carolingians no longer held power. Instead a new family of nobles had seized control: the Ottonians, so called after their most important representative Otto I, a German king from 936 and Emperor of the German Empire from 962 until his death in 973. One of the ways in which the Ottonians sought to bolster their position was through the appointment of bishops, giving these church leaders immense earthly power. The bishop of Utrecht, for example, was not only in charge of the diocese of Utrecht, but also became lord over Sticht (which corresponded roughly with the province of Utrecht today) and Oversticht (now roughly Overijssel and Drenthe). It was thanks to the patronage of the Ottonians that Utrecht became the most important city in the Northern Netherlands. The Church of St Martin that Willibrord had had built was replaced by a huge cathedral in the Romanesque style. Its consecration in 1023 was attended not only by the twelve bishops of the Holy Roman Empire, but also by the Emperor.

One of the bishops appointed by the Ottonians was Ansfridus (995-1010). Bishop Ansfridus presented the Church of St Martin a magnificent manuscript, the so-called Ansfridus Codex. The book is thought to have been made in the monastery at Sankt Gallen, today located in Switzerland (ill. 8).

But once Christianity had finally established itself along the North Sea, the Church faced new problems: the wealth of the its institutions and the tension between spiritual ideals and worldly obligations.

8

Ansfridus codex, St Gallen, around 950-1000; book binding eleventh-thirteenth century with later additions
Based on an inscription on the back of the binding, we know that Bishop Ansfridus (995-1010) presented this codex to The Church of St Martin in Utrecht: 'Decorated with glittering gems and shining gold, I am a gift from Ansfridus to Martin'. Like that of the covers of the Lebuinus codex, the history of the binding of this codex is complicated. What we see now is the result of a restoration dating from around 1500; the original front cover has been lost. For the restoration an old binding from around 1200 was used and subsequently the cross with precious stones and medallions was added. In the four corners we can see the four evangelists.

17

9

Procession crucifix, Maasland, around 1150

During the course of the eleventh century it became common use to place a crucifix on the altar. This crucifix was not only used for that purpose, but also served as a cross for processions. It would be carried into the church atop a long staff at the beginning of Mass before being placed on the altar. Procession crucifixes were also decorated on the back. This crucifix features twining leaves and five medallions on the reverse. Christ has been depicted wearing a crown, as a king who triumphs over death. Above His head the hand of God appears in blessing.

Cloisters and Crusades

Babette Hellemans

10

Holy monk, Northern Netherlands?, 1500-1520
The monk is wrapped in a long robe worn under a cowl with shoulder mantle and hood. His long wide sleeves have been folded back. It is said that the monk represents Bernard of Clairvaux, but the absence of attributes makes it impossible to identify him for certain.

Around the year 1000 northwestern Europe was plagued by Norman raids and other tribal invasions. Although these events seemed 'barbaric', in comparison to the burgeoning Byzantium, the intellectual Middle East and art-loving Spain, it was nevertheless during this period that the first signs of a 'European civilisation' were to emerge. Land reclamation, the growth of cities with their seminaries and universities, all originated during this time. With the spread of Christianity the number of monasteries in the Low Countries increased. In addition, returning crusaders brought back knowledge and expertise from the Holy Land to the West that fostered new insights with regard to hygiene and medical care and led to an upsurge in music and (vernacular) literature.

The monastic culture represented the very core of what would become a 'European civilisation'. A monastery was a place of silence where monks were schooled in the holy language of the Bible. It was essentially a place of learning for all those who sought in seclusion to find God, with at its head an elected abbot, who would ideally lead his monastic community in the way of a mild-mannered, though strict father. The specific nature of the monastic training had a direct influence on the way in which the monks expressed themselves in manuscripts – and thus on the whole way of thinking and writing in the Middle Ages. These manuscripts, sometimes stored in the libraries, were part of the monastery's treasures. Men and women lived apart, with separate convents for women headed by an abbess.

Daily life in the monasteries was highly ordered and regulated, and each monk (ill. 10) or nun of the same order was required to wear identical dress. Saint Benedict of Nursia (†547), founder and abbot of the famous Italian monastery in Monte Cassino, wrote the Rule for Monks, a kind of instruction book for monks in which the rules of the monastic community were recorded. Benedict set down everything: the organisation times for worship and sleep, even the amount to be eaten and drunk. Thanks to its moderation and fellow

11

*Bernulphus codex, Reichenau,
around 1040; binding 13th
century*

This book of the Gospels
was probably an episcopal
gift to the Utrecht Cathedral
(Domkerk). It is not entirely
clear why it has been linked
to the Bishop Bernold
(Bernulphus). The manuscript,
decorated with miniatures, in
any case dates from his time
and originates from the region
of his birth, Southern Germany.
With their richly adorned
covers, such books numbered
among a Cathedral's most
precious possessions. On holy
days they would be borne to
the altar in a procession and
subsequently laid upon it
alongside other church
treasures.

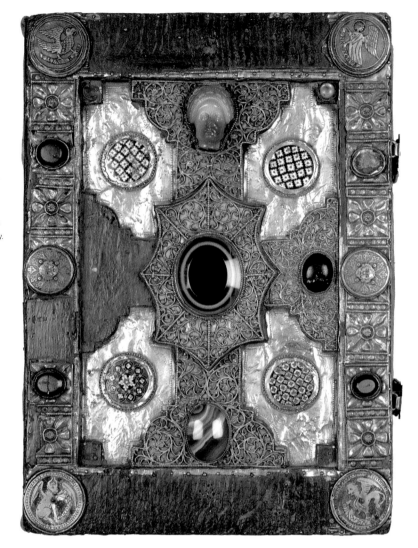

feeling, this Rule was used for centuries as the basis for large parts
of Western monastic life. The taking of the vow was the most
important ritual for someone wishing to enter the monastery; the
novice had to first promise to obey the abbot or abbess. Furthermore
all personal possessions were frowned upon, because humility
before God was all-important. Monks and nuns also had to live
chastely, which meant that sex was strictly forbidden. In addition
prayers were said at no less than eight different times through the
day (known collectively as the hours) and monks gathered together
at the altar where the Eucharist was celebrated. The altar assumed
a central position within the monastic community. In order to
underline its key role, from the eleventh century onwards it
became habitual to place on the altar a cross with on it Jesus Christ
(ill. 9).

In addition monks were expected to work and study hard (ill. 11, 12), for according to the Rule doing nothing was bad for the soul. Being busy meant one fell into a certain kind of rhythm. It was after all not always easy to conform to the secluded monastic life. Hemmed about by all sorts of regulations one lived in a sort of enclave, sometimes totally cut off from the outside world. A body of Cistercian monks, for example, founded a community on Schiermonnikoog, one of the islands in the North Sea shallows off the northern Dutch coast. In fact the name of the island directly reflects their influence: Cistercians were also known in Dutch as *schiermonniken* (grey monks) because of their '*schiere*' (grey or drab) habits of unbleached wool. Gradually, however, the secluded nature of the monastic existence changed, through the contacts the monks maintained with local farmers. Thanks to good crop yields on their lands, some monasteries developed into puissant rich institutions, their abbeys richly

12

Bernulphus codex, Reichenau, around 1040

The monastery in Reichenau where this book of the Gospels was made ranked as one of the top script and illumination centres in Western Europe. The painter of the miniatures in this codex would have had a Byzantine training, as is revealed by the greenish play of shadows across the faces, in the painting of the folds of clothing and in the combination of the primaries red, yellow and blue and the bright blended colours derived from them. St Mark is one of the two evangelists depicted in the manuscript. He is depicted together with his symbol – a winged lion – and is surrounded by prophets and angels.

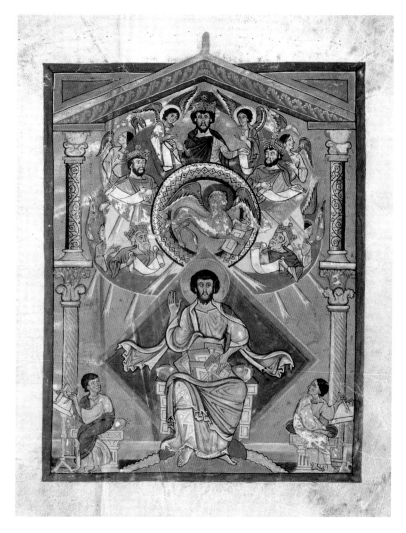

decorated and their treasuries growing ever fuller with gold and precious stones. As time passed, the objections to this way of life grew. It seemed as if the monastic existence had come to more closely resemble that of a worldly life at court, than one based on the ideals of poverty as put forward by Jesus Christ in the Gospels. Sharpest in his critique was Bernard of Clairvaux (†1153), who wrote prolifically about the ideals of the monastic life, directing his ire particularly against the hugely powerful and rich Benedictine monastery of Cluny. 'I cannot believe that your luxuries […] is in keeping with the spirit of our Rule. What counts with you is the richer, the better the worship,' he fulminated.

But society was in a state of extreme flux. The rapid population growth in the late twelfth century meant more and more people flocked to the cities and with them, the monks. Mendicant friars busied themselves intensively with the spiritual care of lay people, particularly with infant baptism and burial of the dead. The most well known mendicant orders were the Franciscans and the Dominicans, named after their founders Francis of Assisi (†1226) (ill. 13) and Dominicus Guzmán of Caleruega (†1221) respectively. The former was to become one of the most influential and well-loved saints. Scion of a rich merchant family, Francis resolved to turn his life around after encountering the wretched conditions in which lepers and the urban poor lived. He took to a life of abject poverty. After he and his twelve companions were recognised as a church body by Pope Innocent III in 1209, Francis was permitted to preach and he went on to found the first Franciscan monastery, near Assisi. Francis' followers called themselves *minores,* which means 'minor' or 'lesser' in Latin. For this reason the followers of these orders were also known as friar minors. A high point in Francis' life was his receiving of the stigmata (literally meaning 'signs') in 1224. In a vision he saw how the wounds sustained by Christ during His death on the cross were etched into his body as holy signs.

Two women played a major role in Francis' life and thereafter. With the widow Domina Jacobea de Settesoli Francis felt at home, viewing her as an equal to the extent that he would address her as 'brother'. Thanks to her position as a woman of nobility, De Settesoli had the means to instruct various artists to portray Francis and he quickly became well-known. The second woman to play an influential role was Chiara ('Clara', †1253) (ill. 14). She fled the family home at the age of 18 and joined the Franciscans. In the monastery at San Damiano she founded a sisterhood of the Franciscan order, the so-called Poor Clares.

Dominicus (ill. 15), founder of the Dominican order, also had strong opinions about the way in which monks should find their way in the world of the city. His family belonged to the Spanish nobility and, as was customary for a boy in such circles, Dominicus read theology at a cathedral school. But while travelling with a friend from Spain through southern France he encountered the Albigensian Crusade being waged to persecute the Cathars. The Crusade was essentially a war against an unorthodox group of

13

Francis of Assisi, Utrecht,
around 1480
Francis of Assisi (1182-1226)
shows his wounds in an appeal
for us to follow Jesus. These
wounds are stigmata, which
appeared in the summer of
1224 on his hands, feet and in
his side after intense meditation
on Jesus' suffering. This sober
lover of nature was a well-
loved saint in the Middle Ages.
Several Dutch examples of
Francis in this pose are still
extant.

14

Clara, Northern Netherlands,
early sixteenth century
Saint Clara (1194-1253) decided
at a young age to devote her life
to God. Secretly she stole from
her parents' house and fled to
Francis of Assisi. For her Francis
founded a second Franciscan
order, the Poor Clares or
Franciscanas. Clara is shown
wearing a double veil and a
cloth fastened under the chin.
Her cloak has been pulled up
under both arms, while her
bare feet are in sandals. In
her right hand Clara is shown
holding a monstrance, a
precious container in which the
host was displayed. Legend
has it that Clara drove out the
Moslims who laid siege to
Assisi in 1240 by showing
them a monstrance.

15

*Mary with child appearing
to St Dominic in a vision,
Utrecht?, first quarter of the
sixteenth century*

The Dominicans worshipped the
Virgin intensively. According to
legend Mary once appeared to
St Dominic and his monks as
they sung a hymn to Mary in
their church. The small dog
flanking St Dominic with a
torch in its mouth refers to
another legend: St Dominic's
mother was said to have
dreamt before he was born that
she had given birth to a dog.
The dog took a torch and set the
world on fire. The story points
to the fiery conviction with
which the Dominicans fought
against heresy. This in turn
earned them the nickname
Domini Canes, that is 'God's
watchdogs'.

16

Saint Christopher, Henrick Douwerman, around 1520-1530

This statue of St Christopher is some two metres tall and one of the biggest medieval statues to have been carved from a single piece of wood that still survives in the Netherlands. In the Middle Ages St Christopher was a popular patron saint of travellers. In many churches his statue was positioned close to the entrance and exit. A glance at St Christopher was thought to shield the faithful against a sudden death.

17

Pilgrim saint, Southern Germany, around 1480-1500

This statue shows us the standard accoutrements of a pilgrim. In his right hand the pilgrim holds a pilgrim's staff. On his head he wears a hat with the brim turned back, on which he can pin his pilgrim's insignia. He has swung a bag on his back. Over his habit, which is gathered into a belt, he wears a wide cloak.

18

Pilgrim's ampoule showing
Thomas Becket and two
knights, Canterbury, last
quarter of the twelfth century

Christians who believed that Evil on earth originated from a demonic alter-ego of the Divine. The Dutch and German word for heretic, 'Ketter' originates from this time, as a corruption of 'Cathar'. The battle against heresy became Dominicus' life's work. As a peripatetic apostle he preached the 'true gospel' and converted people. His followers were consequently also known as Friars Preachers.

Traditional manual labour was replaced by study, with the primary aim of passing on knowledge. The Dominicans played a highly significant role in the development of education in western Europe – Dominicus, for example, ensured that girls, too, could gain an education.

Daily life in the Middle Ages was not circumscribed within the walls of a monastery, village or town: people travelled widely. Not only men but also women took to the road. From accounts passed down we know how difficult such travel could be. Many roads were badly maintained and because few bridges existed, travellers were often forced to take detours of many miles in order to find a suitably shallow crossing place. On average, travellers on foot would journey

19

Reliquary of Thomas Becket,
Limoges, around 1190
This casket in colourful enamel
shows the beheading of the
Archbishop of Canterbury,
Thomas Becket (circa 1118-
1170). His death as a martyr
is depicted on the side of the
reliquary. Behind Thomas
Becket, cross in hand an angel
appears above an altar. The lid
shows the angels transporting
Becket's soul to heaven. Within
two years of his murder, Becket
was declared a saint and his
grave became a well-known site
of pilgrimage. The reliquary was
used to hold relics – remains of
the saint.

Reliquary bust of one of Ursula's companions, Cologne, around 1340-1350

To prepare herself for her impending marriage, Ursula undertook a pilgrimage to Rome. On the return journey she and her fellow travellers were murdered by the Huns near Cologne. This full frontal bust represents one of Ursula's travelling companions. It was used to safe keep bone remains – relics – that served to further strengthen the faithful's sense of her presence. The top of the skull could be flipped up at the front, while three openings in the chest offered a view of the (now missing) relics. The veneration of St Ursula emanated from the St Ursula Church in Cologne, where the relics of Ursula and her companions were displayed in a special chamber. No fewer than 122 similar reliquary busts are to be found there.

some twenty miles a day. The elite – nobility and bishops – travelled on horseback. The biggest danger was brigands. Everywhere, on land and sea, there were highwaymen and pirates. For fear of dying on the journey without having received absolution, travellers often turned to Saint Christopher (ill. 16). Pilgrims journeying to holy places tried to distinguish themselves from travelling salesmen and knights by wearing pilgrim's badges or insignia. It was by these insignia, together with their hat and staff, that people recognised these special travellers (ill. 17). To undertake a pilgrimage to a distant land was taxing and also very expensive. The less well-off tended to journey to places closer by, where popular saints such as Thomas Becket were venerated (ill. 18). A highly popular place of pilgrimage

21

Ursula and her travelling companions, Utrecht, around 1530

According to an 11th century legend, Ursula, the daughter of a Christian king of Great Britain, was asked for her hand in marriage by a pagan prince. She agreed to the union on two conditions: she would first be allowed to undertake a pilgrimage to Rome with 12,000 virgins and the prince would have to convert to the Christian faith. On their return journey the young women, accompanied by the Pope and several cardinals, were set upon by archers of the King of the Huns, and murdered. Only one of their number, St Cunera, escaped death. Here Ursula, somewhat exotically dressed, offers shelter beneath her cloak to eight virgins, the Pope and a cardinal. The colouring of the image is not original, but dates from the seventeenth century.

for the Dutch was Cologne, where the relics of Saint Ursula and her eleven thousand virgins are held. The relics of these saints were kept in magnificent reliquaries (ill. 20, 21), often fashioned from gold and encrusted with precious stones. Such reliquaries would be kept in the treasure house of churches or monasteries, to be displayed during mass and in processions.

Because Jerusalem was regarded as the centre of the world it was by far the most important place of pilgrimage (ill. 22, 25) – not only

22

Model of the Church of the Holy Sepulchre in Jerusalem, Bethlehem, seventeenth century

The first pilgrimages to Jerusalem began after Helena, mother to the Emperor Constantine, found Christ's Cross in 330. Not long after this find, the Church of the Holy Sepulchre was built. The grave and the cross under a single roof brought together the most important events of Christ's last days: His crucifixion and resurrection. For this reason a visit to the Church was the foremost goal of a pilgrimage to the Holy Land.

for Christians, but also for Jews and Moslims. For Jews it was the site where King Solomon's Temple had stood, on Temple Mount. For Moslims Jerusalem ranked second only to Mecca as the most important destination for the *hadj* (Islamic pilgrimage), for it was here that Abraham (Ibrahim) had declared himself willing to sacrifice his son at God's request. Christ died in Jerusalem, and that was the primary reason for Christians to journey there. The Holy Sepulchre was testimony to His suffering, death and resurrection. Pilgrims journeying to the Holy City from Western Europe did so for a range of reasons. Some were doing penance for their sins at a priest's behest, some were believers taking part in the so-called *peregrinatio religiosa* (religious pilgrimage) and others were devout Christians seeking to settle in Jerusalem.

In his call to arms for a holy war in 1095 Pope Urban II combined these ideologies into a new, single holy form of pilgrimage: the crusade. The crusade was not solely a military expedition but also a pilgrimage and thus the crusaders referred to themselves as pilgrims. Of course, the crusades engendered many casualties, particularly on

23

Mother of God Hodegetria,
Constantinople, around 950
Its superior quality indicates
that this ivory icon must have
been carved in one of the best
workshops in Constantinople.
The West and the Byzantine
Empire maintained close
relations during the Middle
Ages, sustained not only by the
emperors but also by traders
and crusaders. It is not known,
however, how this ivory
miniature came to the
Netherlands. The Byzantine
'Hodegetria' icon type of Mary
as 'she who shows the way'
served as a model for the
figures of Mary standing that
began to be made in the West
from around the twelfth century
onwards.

24

Catharijneconvent, view of the south wing

Originally this was a Carmelite monastery. The Carmelites established themselves on the Lange Nieuwstraat in Utrecht in 1468, and immediately started on the construction of a church and monastery. The complex was left unfinished as a result of their enforced departure in 1529. At that time the south wing ran as far as the chapel extension shown in the photograph and was later completed by the St John's Order.

the Moslim side. Furthermore the crusaders were guilty of looting and pillaging on a terrible scale: treasure houses were plundered (ill. 23) and people robbed of their personal belongings. Hospitaller monks and nuns did their best to tend the Christian wounded. One such brotherhood was the Order of the Knights of St John, named after John the Baptist. The Order was a supra-local body, initially headquartered in Jerusalem and later on Cyprus. Quite early on, the Order of the Knights of St John also established a base in Utrecht. A historical source indicates that as early as 1122 there was a brotherhood in Utrecht of which the members referred to them-selves as *Jerosolimitani*, meaning 'those who come from Jerusalem'. The St John's hospital in Utrecht was named after Saint Catherine of Alexandria, the second patron saint of the Order. For more than three centuries the hospitallers carried out their work there, until the Hapsburg Emperor Charles V assumed the worldly powers of the bishop and annexed the building to use it as a prison fortress for incarcerating rebellious Utrecht citizens. This is what we now know as Vredenburg, today, the market place of Utrecht. Eventually the Order of the Knights of St John took up residence in a building (ill. 24), on the Lange Nieuwstraat, today's Museum Catharijne-convent.

Dat · is · die · higuer · vent · b̄

25
Church of the Nativity in Bethlehem with four Jerusalem pilgrims, Amsterdam?, around 1520
These four men had their portraits painted on their return from their pilgrimage to the Holy Land, what is today known as Israel. They are depicted on either side of the cave in Bethlehem where Jesus was born. They bear palm fronds that they took with them from Jerusalem as souvenirs.

Pilgrims returning from the Holy Land – both laypeople and clergy – subsequently often set up a Jerusalem brotherhood. Such brotherhoods existed in various Dutch cities. Often the brotherhood would order a special chapel to be built where its members could ask for Mass to be said. The chapel walls would be decorated with group portraits such as these.

Christ as Man of Suffering, Geertgen tot Sint-Jans, around 1490

This devotional painting, also known as 'Nood Gods' ('God's Extremity') blends together several elements from the story of Christ's suffering. The tortured bleeding Christ bears His Cross. However the wounds in His hands and side indicate He has already been crucified. Mourning angels bear the instruments of His suffering.

Behind the figure of Mary kneeling John the disciple is shown wiping away tears. Pictured left the repentant Mary Magdalene bows over the edge of the tomb. Christ stares out at the viewer as if begging for compassion. The scene is typical of the late medieval experience of faith, which placed a primacy on a strong identification with Christ's suffering.

Meditation and Devotion

3

Babette Hellemans

27

Mourning woman featured in
a representation of the Passion,
Antwerp, around 1480
The edging on the woman's
cloak is inscribed with a hymn
of gratitude, originally sung in
thanks by three youths after
God rescued them from the
flames of a burning oven. In the
Middle Ages people equated this
Old Testament story with the
redemption of the soul through
the crucifixion of Christ.

Christians believe that after death man shall be called to account for the
life he lived on earth. At the end of time Christ the merciful judge will pass
judgement on the souls of men. Looking after one's spiritual welfare was
essential if one was to enter into the kingdom of heaven. In the Middle Ages
this was done by honouring and commemorating the dead. By empathising
with the suffering of Christ, medieval people sought to achieve a place in
heaven. Remembering the dead was the main purpose of art in the period
we now call the Modern Devotion, which emerged at the end of the
fourteenth century in the eastern Netherlands.

Images and representations are important for meditation and
devotion, for they rouse 'the dormant [...] inclination to prayer,'
wrote the Carthusian mystic St John of the Cross (†1591) in his
Ascent of Mount Carmel. And they 'lead the soul via spiritual goods
[...] to the divine union of the soul with God'. Representations were
an aid to meditation (ill. 27). Being a Christian meant believing what
you saw, or more emphatically, 'seeing is believing'. Many decades
prior to this the painter Geertgen tot Sint-Jans had depicted this
notion on a small panel, now regarded as the artistic highpoint of
the Modern Devotion (ill. 26). The painter was inspired by the gospel
of Matthew, which reads: 'Then said Jesus unto his disciples, If any
man will come after me, let him deny himself, and take up his cross,
and follow me' (16:24). The pain is etched into Christ's bloodied
features and His expression of suffering demands the viewer's
attention in a very immediate way. The panel's modest dimensions
mean it is best suited to intimate surroundings, making it an ideal
object for private meditation and devotions. The modern-day viewer
is easily distracted by the host of horrific details, such as the
instruments of torture and the blood flowing everywhere. But that is
not the primary message of the picture. Recent research has shown
that this small painting – and indeed other works of art dating from
this period – should not only be interpreted at a psychological level,
as if people at that time were unnaturally obsessed by death and

macabre scenes. Appearances can be misleading, for devotion centres on the inner meaning of belief, not on its outward trappings. Within the diminutive confines of his painting, Geertgen tot Sint-Jans did not so much depict the pain suffered by Christ as the unimaginable extent of His mercy. Believers meditated on the meaning of this redemptive idea, rather than the bloody tableau before them in their devotions.

Modern Devotion emerged in the eastern Netherlands towards the end of the fourteenth century and refers to a spiritual movement aimed at a simple and sober way of life. The Carthusians were a major source of inspiration for the movement's followers, as was the

28

Commemorative panel showing Christ on the cross, saints and kneeling founders, Northern Netherlands, Utrecht, 1543

The two donors who commissioned the painting are depicted kneeling on either side of the crucified Christ. They are the Benedictine nuns Hadewich van Haredenbroeck and Agnes van Ghent, who lived in the St Steven's Abbey in Oudwijk near Utrecht. Standing behind the two nuns and watching over them are their patron saints. Below the painting an inscription has been added in commemoration: 'Pray for the soul'. Commemorative panels were often to be found in private chapels in the vicinity of the donor's grave.

29

Hymn of praise to Christ, initial showing Bernard hugging the cross, Master of the Bible from Zwolle, around 1480

This fragment comprises a number of formal songs of praise to the suffering Christ. They comprise verse from a long poem on the Passion ascribed to St Bernard of Clairvaux (1091-1153) or his circle. Bernard of Clairvaux was highly regarded in circles of the Modern

Devotion. He was seen as one of the founders of the medieval mystical cult of the Passion, which centred on love for the suffering Christ. The miniature contains a typically mystical representation, in which Christ is flanked by all the appropriate figures but His feet are being hugged by Bernard, who was not present at His crucifixion. In this way the miniature renders St Bernard's immense love for the suffering and death of Christ.

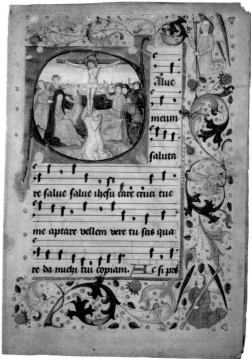

30

Holy family in the carpenter's workshop, Adriaen van Wesel, around 1475-1480

The young Jesus helps His father Joseph in measuring a beam while at the same time listening to Mary reading her prayers aloud, as was customary in the Middle Ages. In this way Jesus combines the contemplative and the active life – ora et labora. A basket of carpenter's tools including a drill and a plane is positioned in the foreground. This group of figures probably formed part of the altar to Mary made by Adriaen van Wesel for the illustrious Brotherhood of Our Lady in 's Hertogenbosch.

mystical work of Bernard of Clairvaux (†1153) (ill. 29) referred to in the previous chapter and the methodical thought on Christ's suffering of the Franciscan Bonaventure (†1274). Another inspirational text was the widely available rendition of the hundred points of meditation put forward by the German Dominican Henricus Soso (†1366). Geert Grote (†1384) is seen as 'the father of the Modern Devotion'. Initially he embarked on an ecclesiastical career but after a series of personal successes – a classic tale – he became seriously ill and renounced his former ways. At a time when ecclesiastical pomp and circumstance and the worldly ways of many clerics gave offence, Grote called for repentance, prayer and sober living in the way of Christ, preaching his message as he journeyed from town to town. The church authorities regarded this vision on the faith as a criticism of their own way of thinking and consequently saw Grote as a threat. Quite quickly he was banned from preaching. But Grote did not give in and continued his work via the written word, among other things by translating prayers for daily use from the Latin. This in particular played an extraordinarily large role in his rapid rise to fame.

Geert Grote and his followers sought after a personal form of spirituality, founded on meditation (ill. 35) and prayer. Particularly well known are Grote's sermons on the Birth of Our Lord (*Sermo de nativitate Domini*) in which he posits that 'through representation (ill. 28, 30, 32) the eyes of believers slowly become accustomed, so that they will not be blinded by the bright light' (r. 85-87). In circles around Grote, which after his death congregated in the vicinity of Windesheim near Zwolle, the Bible would be read aloud during meals. Difficult passages were clarified, and prayers were also read aloud.

Manuscripts

Prior to the invention of printing (around 1450), books were hand written. Such books are known as manuscripts, from the Latin manus (hand) and scriptum (written). The material written on was parchment, made from animal hides. Thanks to the sheep's thick wool, sheep hides were popular because these tended to have suffered less damage as a result of wounds from prickly shrubs and undergrowth. To make a single codex – the type of book we still use today – an entire herd was required. Together with the sometimes highly valuable raw materials required for the paint used for the miniatures, this made books into extremely rare objects having considerable prestige.

The copier was almost always anonymous and monks in the scriptorium, a separate room within the monastery walls, almost always executed the writing.

From the twelfth and thirteenth centuries onwards, books were no longer only transcribed by monks, but also by lay people. Initially this occurred primarily in the area flanking the Theology Faculty in Paris and Boulogne's Law Faculty. Here professional studios sprang up, workshops in which various writers and sometimes also special artists for the illustrations (miniatures) were involved in the production process. In the late Middle Ages the Low Countries became known for their extremely costly books of hours, or breviaries, made for personal use and often richly illuminated with extensive series of miniatures. One such breviary is that made for Beatrijs of Assendelft (ill. 29, 44).

31

Book of Hours, Annunciation, Delft, around 1495

With messenger's staff in hand the Angel Gabriel appears to the Virgin Mary to announce the birth of Jesus. In a ray of light a dove descends, symbolic of the Holy Ghost. The right hand page shows the beginning of the divine offices of Our Lady. Books of Hours, or breviaries, were written for individual worship. As the name implies, they contained prayers for fixed hours of the day. They were extremely costly primarily because of their magnificent illuminations, small or page-filling representations of the birth and the Passion of Christ, the Last Judgement, saints and other subjects. The margins of the text and miniatures were decorated with many coloured leaves, flowers and animals.

32

Seated Christ Child, Mechelen?, early sixteenth century

As saviour of the world Christ lifts His right hand in a gesture of blessing. The globe in his left hand derives from the imperial orb that had symbolised worldly power since Roman times. In the Middle Ages images of the Christ child were used in different ways. On feast days, for example, and particularly at Christmas, monks but also lay people would dress up the images and put them on display.

33

Apostle Paul, Arnt from Kalkar
from Zwolle, around 1475
The large, slightly slanted eyes
give Paul, the 'apostle of the
heathen', a melancholy
expression. The book he holds
refers to his writings. In his
other hand, now missing, he
held the sword with which he
was beheaded.

34

Diptych showing scenes from the life of Christ, Northern France or Flanders, around 1375

Four tableaux depict respectively the birth of Christ, His instruction in the temple, the adoration of the Magi and His crucifixion. In the fourteenth century ivory relief carvings of this nature depicting both religious and non-religious scenes were manufactured in great numbers.

35

Gethsemane group, Worms? around 1440

The evening before He was condemned to death Christ went to the Garden of Gethsemane with three of His disciples: Peter, James and John. There He prayed that the cup of suffering might pass from Him (Matthew 26). The disciples fell asleep. The statues were originally positioned in a realistic landscape at the back of the church or in a chapel in the churchyard. The group of statues was intended to inspire the faithful in their meditations on Christ's suffering.

After Geert Grote's death, Thomas à Kempis (†1471) was to become the most influential writer of the Modern Devotion with his 'bestseller' *The imitation of Christ*. Even today, Thomas à Kempis is one of the most widely read Christian authors. He became the leader of a community known as the Brethren of the Common Life, which was later to become world-famous. Its members were not only clerics, but also laypeople. They lived as monks and nuns in poverty, chastity and obedience and according to a community rule. The fact that they determined to live this life at home, either singly or together, was the reason they dit not take monastic vows. Further-more they were not permitted to beg for alms and were deemed to take care of their daily needs through manual labour.

During the era of Modern Devotion, meditation played a central role (ill. 36). Meditation was seen as a pilgrimage wherein step by step one commemorated events from the life of Jesus. A thorough knowledge of the Bible was necessary in order to do so, and thus the story was simplified in order to render meditations suitable for those with little education. So it is that the inside of this diptych depicts (ill. 34) tableaux taken from the life of Christ at four 'key moments': His birth, Jesus in the Temple, the Wise Men worshipping

36

Veronica and the grieving women beneath the cross, Brussels?, around 1475

These images have been carved from the same block of wood and come from the same altar-piece depicting scenes from the Passion of Christ. Veronica has just received the sweat cloth from Jesus as He passed by, with on it the imprint of His face. Mary, mother of Jesus, reaches out to the cross that was probably positioned in between the women. Mary Magdalene is recognisable as a penitent sinner by her hair hanging down. On the right is one of the other women who were often portrayed in representations of the crucifixion or of Christ being taken down from the cross. Their attitude, gestures and tear-stained faces are expressive of their immense grief.

37

Gregorian mass, Master of the Spring of Life, around 1510
The painting depicts the legend of Christ's appearance to Pope Gregory the Great (540-604) during the celebration of Mass.

Christ is shown as the Man of Suffering in his grave. He is surrounded by the instruments of the Passion, which help the viewer to identify with His suffering. The celebration of the

Mass serves to commemorate how Christ sacrificed Himself on the cross to absolve us from our sins, enabling those who believe in Him to gain life eternal. Each Mass was thought to redeem a

soul from purgatory. It was from this belief that the custom arose of having a mass – a Gregorian mass — said for the deceased each day for the first thirty days after their death.

Christ and His death on the Cross. In a church or monastery one could 'meditate' on the life of Christ whilst walking the ambulatories and drawing inspiration from the sometimes life-sized figures (ill. 33) depicting His life. In such ways the layman also gained access to the stories from the gospels (ill. 38) and was able to imagine Christ's suffering, the Passion of Christ. In addition prayers to Mary, mother of God and the saints offered protection and functioned as some sort of preparation for death. This was vitally important because people believed that as soon as you died, the soul left the body, bound for heaven, hell or purgatory. No matter what the adversity, there was always a saint on whom the believer could call for aid. As such the need to commemorate the dead played an important role in everyday life, and not only on All Souls. For even if the person in question had already passed away, he or she could still benefit from prayer, which served to shorten the soul's sojourn in purgatory. Burial rites, the tolling of the bells, the observation of nightly wakes and services of devotion all spurred people on to pray for the souls of the dead (ill. 37). Those who were wealthy enough would pay for masses to be said in which the dead could be commemorated for as long as forty days.

Alongside the Passion, scenes from Christ's youth formed the main subject in the art of the time. Understandably His mother

38

Shield on the cope of David of Burgundy, Northern Netherlands, Utrecht?, late - fifteenth century

David of Burgundy, bishop of Utrecht, commissioned this cope to be made, subsequently gifting it to the collegiate church of the Janskerk in Utrecht. The shield is decorated with a representation of the resurrection of Christ, embroidered in silk and gold thread. On either side two prior depictions have been added of stories from the Old Testament: Jonah being spewed out by the whale and Samson bearing away the walls of Gaza.

39

Head and shoulders of a Mary figure, Master of the Utrecht Woman's Head in Stone, first quarter of the sixteenth century

This stone head forms part of a representation of the annunciation, the heralding of Jesus' birth. The representation, displayed in a church in Utrecht, was by an anonymous maker who derives his makeshift name from this particular fragment. The artist was the leading sculptor working in Utrecht in the period from roughly 1490 to 1525. The 'meester' or master probably had a major workshop with large-scale production. Statues from his workshop were even exported as far afield as Norway. Typical of this particular sculptor are oval faces with a double chin, a high, rounded forehead and half-moon eyes with wrinkles beneath. The high shaven forehead was fashionable at the time.

Techniques in sculpture

In spite of the second of the Biblical Ten Commandments which decrees that man shall not make any graven image, sculpture flourished in the Middle Ages. Frequently the church saw it as the most effective medium for exhorting the faithful to follow a pious life, and church buildings were amply furnished with statues of the saints. The most valuable and costly works were kept in the most important place in the church building, at the altar. Such works are called altarpieces. Statues were hewn from stone or carved from wood. These two techniques differ greatly from one another.

Stone is a material that is difficult to work, and depending on the type of stone different types of cutting techniques had to be learned. Stone does however reflect the light in a particularly subtle way (ill. 39). In wooden figures the effect is entirely different – wood absorbs the light. In addition the material could be worked far faster than stone with the result that in the Middle Ages most of the statues were carved from wood.

The Medieval sculptor had no guild – there were too few of them for that. Instead they tended to join related guilds in a city, such as the goldsmiths' guild, for example. Sculptors in the Netherlands mostly made use of the hardy, and therefore longlasting, oak. The best wood would not have any knots, as this was obviously important in order to achieve an even surface. The carver's biggest fear however was that the wood bought was not dry enough and risked splitting, because wood shrinks as it dries out. The sculptor would start by driving chisels and gouges into the wood with a hammer, but as the image took shape so his tools would become finer and more precise. Finally the statue would be sanded down. But after sanding the statue was still unfinished: most wooden statues in the Middle Ages were painted and gilded. We call this 'polychrome' or 'embellishment'. This was the task of the painter, although there were some sculptors who did it themselves. Sometimes the statues were not only painted, but were given a crown or embellished with precious stones or pieces of glass. The transition to Protestantism in 1581 spelled the demise of the profession. Because Protestantism forbade the use of statues in churches, no new commissions came for the carving of religious statues, commissions on which the carvers had relied almost exclusively for their livelihood.

40

Mary with child, Maasland, around 1275

This particular Mary is a rare example of early Gothic polychrome sculpture. Mary and child look rather solemn and stiff. Jesus is more of an adult in miniature than a realistic looking infant. The image is quite crudely carved and the base coat for the painting is thick.

41

'Anna-te-drieën' (St Anne with Mary and the infant Jesus), Mechelen, around 1520

Anne is the mother of Mary and grandmother to Christ. In the late Middle Ages she was held up as the shining example for women to follow as mother and wife. As a widow, too, she had led an exemplary life. For this reason she was not only patroness of married women, but widows too. The statue still boasts its original ornate decoration. The hem of Anne's golden cloak has been decorated with punched holes. Mary wears a small lead crown. The 'Queen of Heaven' holds her child Jesus who reaches out to the book in St Anne's hand.

42

Mary on the grassy bank,
Northern Netherlands, around
1480-1500

Humbly seated on a grassy
bank, Mary breastfeeds her
child. The roses surrounding the
garden – hortus conclusus –
symbolise her virginal state. In
countless songs of praise and
other religious texts Mary is
compared to a rose. The bright
halo of light surrounding
mother and child is symbolic
of Mary's holiness and Christ's
divinity.

43

Annunciation, Middle Rhine
region, around 1410

The panel forms part of the side
leaves of a large painted altar-
piece. On Sundays and feast
days the inside leaves would
be opened, to reveal tableaux
from the life of Mary on a gold
background. The closed shutters
were decorated with scenes
from the Passion of Christ, not
all of which have been preserved. The stories so depicted
instructed believers in the history of the faith and directed their
thoughts to the spiritual.

47

*Breviary belonging to Beatrijs
of Assendelft, Delft, around
1485*

*A breviary is a book of prayer
for priests, nuns and monks.
This particular one was
probably made to mark the
entry of Beatrijs of Assendelft to
the St Maria ter Zijl convent in
Haarlem. Her parents concluded
a contract for the entry of their
daughter into the convent in
1485. Due to her poor health
she was exempted from a
number of compulsory daily
duties and tasks in the convent.
Consequently the breviary
contains no prayers for the
night. The miniatures and the
marginalia have been executed
by three different masters. In
this miniature we see Beatrijs
kneeling before church father
Augustine (354-430) whose
rules for living the nuns
followed.*

was afforded a major role. Initially Mary (ill. 40, 41) was linked to
Christ, but towards the end of the Middle Ages a veneration of the
Virgin Mary emerged that became increasingly independent of the
events in Christ's life. Although she is pictured together with Christ
in this representation (ill. 42), the theme is centred on Mary. She is
seated in an enclosed or walled garden (*hortus conclusus*), a typically
medieval concept which emphasised her virginity and thus her
purity. In the late Middle Ages the life of Mary, her birth, life with
Christ and her death increasingly became the focus of interest.

This highlight from the museum's collection, a medieval altar-
piece (ill. 43) from the Middle Rhine region, would have been placed
on the altar. The shutters depict scenes from the Passion on one
side, but the other side is devoted entirely to Mary. Because the side
depicting tableaux from Mary's life was only displayed on holy days,
the quality of the pigment is exceptional, enabling us to see how
extremely fine the artists' brushstrokes were. The same holds true
for this extremely ornate breviary (ill. 44) a highpoint of Northern
Netherlandish manuscript. It was made for the young gentlewoman
Beatrijs van Assendelft to mark her entry into the St Maria ter Zijl
Convent in Haarlem. This sophisticated representation, with its
fine eye for detail and painstakingly rendered faces, depicts Beatrijs
kneeling in front of Augustine. The volume is worthy of Beatrijs'
noble antecedents, so that she could take part in the convent's
official prayers with justifiable pride. But the influence of Modern
Devotion and – insofar as one can generalise – the Middle Ages does
not cease with this chapter. For the humanist Erasmus was very
much a child of this school. In Deventer he was taught by Johannes
Scynten, one of the Brethren of the Common Life. Erasmus,
humanism and everything to which it gave birth, form the subject
of the following chapters.

Humanism and Reformation

Tanja Kootte

Humanism and Reformation

45

Desiderius Erasmus, copy after Quinten Matsijs, latter half of the sixteenth century

This portrait shows the scholar Erasmus in bonnet and gown, writing in his study. The work is a copy after a painting executed on commission in 1517 by Quinten Matsijs.

At the beginning of the sixteenth century there was but one church, the Roman Catholic Church (ill. 46, 47). While there had always been people critical of this church, it had never resulted in a radical breakaway. In the sixteenth century that was all to change. Thanks to the invention of printing, people came into contact with other ideas, which led eventually to the emergence of different churches and different schools of thought. Would they be able to co-exist in a spirit of tolerance?

Nowadays, death for some signifies the end of existence. Others believe in a life after death, although no-one knows what that would be like. In the sixteenth century, when poor harvests and epidemics meant death was a constant companion, almost all people believed there was more to life than just this existence on earth; they believed in a heaven and a hell. After death everyone would be called to account for their life before God. And who could help you on this day of final judgement?

The official teaching was that no one could be saved but through the church. Of course there had been criticism of the church down the centuries, such as that levelled at the way of life of those in holy orders, or the opposition against certain articles of faith or practices. In his famous work *Lof der Zotheid* (In Praise of Folly), for example, the scholar Desiderius Erasmus (1469-1536) (ill. 45) mocked the exaggerated veneration of the saints. 'Is it not foolish … that the one saint has to help against toothache and the other has to return stolen goods?' Erasmus wanted to purge the church of superstition and unnecessary ceremony. He wanted a return to the source: the Bible. With this aim he published a critical edition of the New Testament.

Erasmus is the most well-known exponent of Biblical humanism, which propagated a marriage between Christianity and the rediscovered classical Greek and Roman cultures (ill. 46). Biblical stories were to serve as guidelines for living a pious life. Biblical

46
Tabernacle, Southern
Netherlands, around 1550
The architecture of this
tabernacle, which held
consecrated wafers, was clearly
inspired by that of the Roman
triumphal arch. Rather than
an imperial victory it is the
Eucharist that is being exalted,
through classical conventions
pressed into the service of
Christianity.

texts became better known through prints and paintings, cupboards and household objects, such as this stained glass pane (ill. 48) depicting the deterrent of a devastated Sodom and Gomorrah, with in the foreground the pious and obedient patriarch Abraham.

For all his criticisms, Erasmus remained within the Roman Catholic Church. In Germany, however, a radical schism opened up. Like Erasmus, the Augustinian monk Martin Luther (1483-1546) (ill. 49) devoted himself to a study of the Bible and he, too, posed the question of how man could be saved. He sought the answer in the Bible, which he considered so important that he translated it into the vernacular. Luther believed that everyone should be in a position to read the Bible, for it was in the Bible that he had found the answer to his question. Contrary to the teachings of the Church

47

Crook of the bishop's staff belonging to Aegidius de Monte, Antwerp, 1570

This crown atop a bishop's staff was crafted on commission for Aegidius de Monte, the first bishop of the then diocese of Deventer. In the centre of the crook is a diminutive statue of St Lebuinus, a missionary of the eastern Netherlands in the eighth century and since then regarded as the patron saint of Deventer.

48

Abraham surveys the devasta-tion of Sodom, design Jacob Cornelisz. van Oostsanen, around 1520

Abraham the patriarch surveys the burning city of Sodom. His nephew Lot extended hospitality to two angels. When Lot's fellow citizens turned on the two strangers, the cities of Sodom and Gomorrah were laid waste. Lot was spared.

49

Martin Luther, Lucas Cranach,
1546

Many portraits have been made
of Martin Luther, particularly by
his friend, Lucas Cranach. Given
this portrait is dated 1546 and
inscribed vivus docet ('in life
he taught') it was made in the
year that Luther died.

50

Parable of the Good Shepherd,
Northern Netherlands?, 1581

In John 10, Jesus likens Himself
to the Good Shepherd who
enters the fold by the door. But
he that does not enter by the
door into the fold, but climbs up
some other way, Jesus warns,
is a thief and a murderer. This
satirical painting depicts Jesus
standing in the doorway of the
fold, while Roman Catholic
priests attempt to scale its roof.

51

Weighing scales of the true religion, Netherlands, first half of the seventeenth century

The hand of God holds a pair of scales in which a number of reformers, including Luther and Calvin, have laid a Bible. On the other side the Pope and other Catholic priests look on as their liturgical plate is shown to lack equal weight.

it was not through good works that man could be saved but only by the grace of God (Romans 1:17): 'The righteous will live by faith'.

Thanks to the invention of printing and better education, more people came into contact with Luther's ideas. They read his countless pamphlets, sermons and theological works. In addition Luther had an eye for the power of images: innumerable cartoons and paintings by his followers disseminated his ideas (ill. 51).

The painting *Image of the Good Shepherd* (ill. 50), for example, depicts Roman Catholic priests coming down like wolves upon the fold – that is to say as robbers and murderers. The diminutive panel (ill. 52) shows a portrait of the pope, which on being turned over turns out to be a devil.

In the eyes of the church and of the Holy Roman Emperor Charles V, Luther was an apostate and a heretic. The Emperor saw it as his Christian duty to oppose Luther's teachings, also in the Netherlands, which fell under his control. Strict proclamations attempted to prevent the dissemination of the new doctrine.

In 1526 Jacob van Liesvelt published the first illustrated Bible (ill. 53) in the Low Countries, based on parts of the Holy Scripture translated by Luther. But Van Liesvelt's Bibles were viewed with suspicion by the authorities. In 1536 his stock of reformational texts was confiscated and burnt and later Van Liesvelt himself was arrested and executed in 1545.

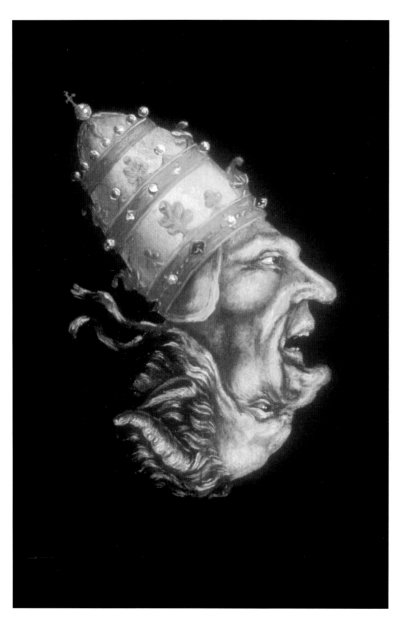

Satirical cartoon mocking
the Pope, Netherlands (?),
seventeenth century
When this panel is turned
180 degrees, the representation
changes. The Pope becomes
the devil; the devil, the Pope.
This representation, like many
satirical paintings, derives
originally from a print.

Satire in service of the true faith

The pope a devil? Luther a heretic, struggling in the sea? By means of satirical cartoons Protestants and Catholics tried to convince one another that they were right. Luther and his followers in particular were well aware of the possibilities offered by such missives. Printed cartoons were not particularly
costly, so they could be distributed on a large scale. Some representations were also rendered as paintings and bear witness to the passion with which the rival groups opposed one another.

Museum Catharijneconvent has a unique collection of these satirical works.

53

The so-called Liesvelt Bible,
Antwerp, Jacob van Liesvelt,
1532
In 1526 Jacob van Liesvelt
published the first complete
and illustrated Bible in the
Netherlands. This Bible is
based on Luther's translation
while the illustrations are also
taken from Luther's Bible.

54

Head of a Christ figure,
Kleef-Gelre, anonymous,
latter half fifteenth century
This head comes originally
from a so-called Holy Grave,
a Medieval group of statues in
which Jesus was shown in an
open coffin, surrounded by His
grieving loved ones. This head
is quite badly damaged because
it lay in the Meuse River for a
long period of time before it was
dredged up near Ravenstein.

When Charles V ceded the government of the Low Countries to his son Philip II of Spain in 1555, it was in the belief that the heresy was as good as under control. Even so, Philip II continued the persecution of heretics unabated, which greatly fuelled the discontent among the Dutch. The population asked themselves whether it was necessary to keep persecuting people for their faith and to execute them because of their beliefs.

The steadfast belief and piety shown by the persecuted evoked the sympathy of large parts of the population. The fate of the persecuted 'Protestants' evoked compassion, also from the Catholic faithful who still made up the greater part of the Dutch population. Freedom of conscience became an important principle in the Low Countries (ill. 56).

'Protestants' was a name applied not only to Luther's followers but also to the so-called 'Baptists'. The Baptists also studied the Bible closely and only allowed themselves to be baptised after a personal confession of faith. Alongside these two groups there also existed an ever-growing group of followers of another reformer, John Calvin. Contrary to Luther's tenets of obedience to the government, these Calvinists believed that under certain circumstances it was justifiable to rise in revolt. And that is also what happened in the Netherlands.

In early August 1566 the powder keg ignited, due in part also to the dire economic conditions of the time. Fierce Calvinists in Flanders stripped the churches of their – to Calvinist eyes – sacrilegious images and altars, missals and liturgical garments and sometimes even of their windows and organs (ill. 54). In the latter half of August, the churches in Ghent, Antwerp and Dutch cities became targets. This iconoclasm left a lasting impression. The pious Catholic king Philip II was incensed at this sacrilegious movement. He dispatched the Spanish Duke of Alva to the Low Countries. Some nobles were put to death and Stadtholder William the Silent was forced to flee; his possessions were confiscated. In the ensuing years William the Silent orchestrated the rebellion against Spain – a fight for freedom and for tolerance. He strove for freedom of worship for both Catholic and Protestant, although in the end this ideal remained unrealised. The colourful painting *The tyranny of Alva* (ill. 55) by Dirck van Delen may effectively be seen as a summary of the motivation behind the Dutch uprising against the Spanish king. The Spanish Duke of Alva is seated beneath a canopy with at his feet a flurry of torn and tattered documents, signifying the broken laws and revoked privileges in the Low Countries. The text of the volume bottom right reads, significantly, RELIGIE WERT.VER/DRVCKT (religion was repressed). The 17 Dutch provinces kneel before the throne, personified as 17 women.

    The memory of Alva, who lost his 'bril' ('glasses' in Dutch, but here a pun on Brielle) on April 1, 1572, persists to this day in a string of jokes. The Low Countries threw off the yoke of the Spanish king and freedom of conscience became a central tenet within the new Republic of the Seven United Provinces. This right was even officially enshrined in a sort of constitution, the Union of Utrecht (1579): 'No one may be persecuted for their conscience'.

56 *(pp 60-61)*

Moses with the tablets, encircled by two families, Maarten de Vos, Antwerp, 1574/75.
The centre of this group portrait of an Antwerp family depicts the Biblical story of Moses showing *the Ten Commandments to the people of Israel on Mount Sinai. (Exodus:34). The man who commissioned the painting, Peter Panhuys, is shown second from right in the row of men. He was* *a member of a circle of scholars, artists and notables who called for religious tolerance and a deeper, more meaningful experience of faith that emanated from obedience to God's laws.*

Ick bē die Heere v Godt
Die v wt eghipten lant
wt de dienſthuyſe hebbe
Gheleydt ghy en ſult gheen
ander ghode hebbē neffens
my ghy en ſult v ghee hedde
noch enighe ghelyckenſſe ...
makē van eenige darbouen
inde herrel is noch van
datter op die aerde is of
vā datter inder wateren
is onder der aerden en aā
hidtſe noch en dieē ſe niet
want ick die Heere v Go
ben ∙&∙
Ghy en ſole den naem des
Heeren uws Godts niet
te vergeefs ghebruyke

&∙
Syt gedachtich den
ſebaoth dagh dat ghy
heylicht ſes dagen ſu
aerbeyden en al v w
doen maer dr ſeuenſt
is den ſebaoth des H
uws Gods ∙&∙

Piety and Enlightenment

Tanja Kootte

57

Interior of the Grote Kerk in Alkmaar, Pieter Saenredam, 1635

Pieter Saenredam is famous for his church interiors, which he rendered as highly realistic representations. This set him apart from earlier painters of architecture, whose interiors were largely based on fantasy. However Saenredam has added an element to this painting that would never have been found in the Grote Kerk in 1635: a baroque altar with a man kneeling before it.

The new Republic harboured a diverse range of religious beliefs. A single church was privileged: the Dutch Reformed Church. But at the same time there was a right to freedom of conscience (ill. 58): no one was to be adversely affected in their private life on account of their beliefs. This relative freedom attracted many foreign dissenters to the Netherlands.

The Calvinists' church, the Reformed Church, took over from the Roman Catholic Church. As a 'public' church it was to serve all the inhabitants of a village or town. In the church people could marry or have their children baptised (ill. 59) and, until the nineteenth century, that same building was also where people were buried.

The reformers gained control over the existing medieval churches, which they adapted for their services of worship by stripping them of their images and altars. For this reason this small painting by Pieter Saenredam, *Interior of the Grote or Sint-Laurenskerk at Alkmaar* (ill. 57) is so special. In the beautiful church interior a man kneels before an altar, while in the nave the statues can still be seen. Roman Catholic attributes of this kind no longer featured at all in Protestant churches, and in this case Saenredam was probably working on commission for a Catholic patron.

In Protestant churches pride of place was given to the pulpit from which the minister would preach the Word. Twice on Sundays and also during the week the minister – generally a university graduate – would preach a sermon. In an era without radio or television, his influence was great. It was not uncommon for a minister to attract listeners not only from among his own circle but also others, who came to services out of interest.

In the painting by the artist from Weesp Gijsbert Sibilla (ill. 60) we can see the canopied pews opposite the pulpit, intended for members of the city council. For those having ambitions to public office were expected to be members of the official, reformed church.

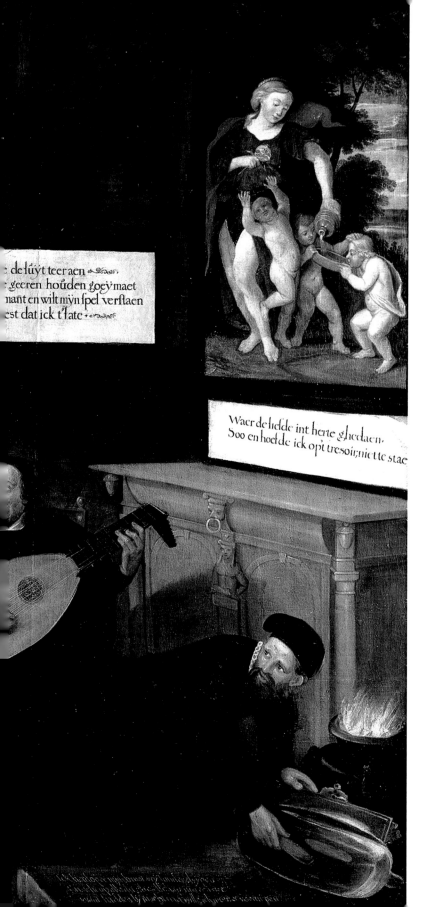

: de luyt teer aen ⚬⚭
: geeren houden goey maet
nant en wilt mijn spel verstaen
est dat ick t'late ⚬⚭

Waer de liefde int herte ghedaen,
Soo en hoefde ick op't tresoir niet te staen

58

*Peace exhorts the churches
to be tolerant, Northern
Netherlands, first quarter
seventeenth century*

Luther (with lute), Calvin (with
a 'fine calf') and the Pope (with
a cat, from 'cat licks') appear to
be sitting at table together like
brothers. An Anabaptist (shown
dipping his bread a second time)
kneels in a corner. The female
figure on the left, representing
Peace, exhorts those present to
keep the peace.

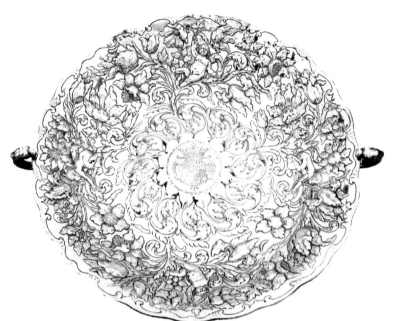

59

Baptismal charger from the Reformed Church in Bergen, David Micheel, The Hague, 1658

For a long period this magnificent dish was used as a baptismal font, later it was also used as a bread dish during Holy Communion. The Egmont family is thought to have gifted the dish to the church in memory of their daughter Hester, who died young.

60

Interior of the Grote Kerk or Laurentius Church in Weesp, Gijsbert Sibilla, around 1635

This unusual painting combines church interior with group portrait. The woman pictured in the foreground right suckles her child. In the same way believers were to imbibe God's word like mother's milk.

61

Family saying grace before the meal, Northern Netherlands, 1627

The members of this God-fearing family fold their hands at a decked table. A vine grows in through the window on the left, in reference to Psalm 128: 'Blessed is every one that feareth the Lord… happy shalt thou be, and it shall be well with thee. Thy wife shall be as a fruitful vine by the sides of thine house'.

62

Majolica plate, circa 1620
This plate is an early example of the way in which wealthy Dutch people would decorate their houses with pious texts. Plates such as these were intended to decorate a room, positioned over the lintel of a door or on the mantlepiece.

63

Baptism of the Eunuch,
Rembrandt van Rijn, 1626
This colourful painting is a
youthful work by Rembrandt,
inspired by the work of his
master, Peter Lastman. The
scene is based on Acts chapter
8. A eunuch from the Ethiopian
court asks Philip to baptise him
after Philip instructed him in
the Bible.

But far from everyone was a member of the Reformed Church. Alongside the Dutch Reformed Church, there were, broadly speaking, two other major religious denominations in the Netherlands: the Roman Catholics and the Baptists. In addition there were a string of smaller groupings, such as the Lutherans. For a long period of time there were people who held back from joining or definitively committing themselves to one or other of these groupings. But that did not mean such people had turned away from the faith: on the contrary, many Dutch had a lively interest in religion.

The Biblical world formed part of daily life. Biblical scenes and pious texts were depicted on gable stones and also frequently served to decorate household objects such as cupboards, blanket boxes and crockery (ill. 62). In the parlour of the family in prayer at table, dressed in black with hands folded (ill. 61) we see on closer examination a grapevine growing in through the window. This is a reference to the blessed man in Psalm 128, of whom it is said that his 'wife shall be as a fruitful vine...'

Protestants and Catholics alike had a penchant for scenes from the Old and New Testaments. In his early years Rembrandt painted

64

Gideon's sacrifice, Ferdinand
Bol, 1640
With his staff the angel sets the
meal that Gideon has prepared
for him ablaze. Gideon starts
backwards, frightened. This
theme was a favourite subject
for artists of Rembrandt's
circle because it offered the
opportunity to portray an
extreme emotion such as a
shock. This is a youthful work
by one of Rembrandt's most
talented students, Ferdinand
Bol.

65

*A penitent David chooses
between three plagues, Pieter
Fransz. de Grebber, 1635-40*
The Haarlem-based painter
Pieter de Grebber regularly
drew inspiration from
Rembrandt – here the face of
King David has been modelled
on an etching by Rembrandt.
The aging King David has sinned
and must choose between three
punishments: famine (the barren
ears of corn), war (the sword)
or pestilence (the skull).

66

States Bible, Wed. J. van Someren, Amsterdam 1684

Following the publication of the States Bible translation in 1637, demand for illustrated versions grew. To meet the demand printers kept a store of prints from which the customer could make a selection. The prints chosen were then bound along with the text. This magnificent two-volume edition contains 150 coloured engravings.

Baptism of the Eunuch (ill. 63), a panel in which the colours are so bright that not many people would immediately identify it as a work by the Old Master. Executed in warm sepia tints, *The Sacrifice of Gideon* (ill. 64) is far more in keeping with Rembrandt's later work and as such is an example of his influence on one of his most successful pupils, Ferdinand Bol. The theme of Gideon was a favourite subject in Rembrandt's circles because it offered an opportunity to portray an extreme of emotion. Also full of emotion is the wonderful old King David, depicted in full regalia but at the same time in an attitude of acute penitence by the Haarlem painter Pieter de Grebber (ill. 65).

The significance of the Bible, in church but also at school, was recognised by the government. For this reason it supported the realisation of a new translation (1626-1637) that was to become known as the 'Statenvertaling' (States translation) (ill. 66). This translation – still in use today in certain Dutch Reformed circles – was an immediate success and had a major impact on Dutch language and culture. Popular references to the Eleven Towns skating marathon as the 'expedition of all expeditions', for example, are modelled on Biblical syntactical constructions such as 'vanity of all vanities' or 'the God of gods'.

Biblical painting in the circle of Rembrandt

Stories full of drama are what thrilled painters in the seventeenth century. The big Bible stories and those of mythology were favoured subjects. The highpoint was the point at which the protagonist was seized by an excess of emotion as a result of a sudden change of circumstance. His response – fright, wonder, grief – had to be depicted in a convincing manner. Particularly painters in the circle of Rembrandt were highly accomplished in the depiction of such dramatic events.

The decision to undertake a new translation of the Bible was taken at the so-called Synod of Dordrecht. This church synod in 1618/19 was attended by domestic and foreign representatives of the Reformed churches. The reason for coming together was a theological difference of opinion which arose among Reformed believers at the beginning of the seventeenth century.

The satirical cartoon included here (ill. 67) depicts the theological position of the strictly orthodox reformers. They accused their opponents, the moderates or Remonstrants, of embracing a theological stance that tended towards Catholicism. In the painting *The Arminian muck wagon* Remonstrants and Catholics are shown fraternally side by side in a single carriage, which is hitched to horses both front and back. But whatever direction the wagon ultimately takes, it will pulverise the Bible lying beneath.

The Remonstrant ministers were eventually forced to leave the country. They founded a new church community: the Remonstrant Brotherhood (1619). Later, in a more forgiving social climate, they were able to return to the Netherlands. But they met more or less in secret, in church buildings not recognisable as such and known as 'schuilkerken' ('hidden churches').

Roman Catholic believers were already well-acquainted with the hidden church. Catholics had become a distinct minority and their church buildings had been confiscated. Although freedom of conscience was still valid, this did not mean Catholics were openly able to conduct or attend Mass. For this reason they initially met in small places of worship at one another's houses and later in larger, but not openly identifiable churches. As late as 1656 the priest

67

Arminian Muck Wagon,
Essaias van de Velde (circle of),
around 1625

Beneath a louring sky, Roman
Catholic and Remonstrant clergy
sit together in a farmer's wagon,
wanting to head in opposite
directions. But whatever
direction the wagon ultimately
takes, it will pulverize the Bible
lying beneath it. The painter
obviously believed both groups
were in the wrong.

68

*Nicolaas Stenius, Frans Hals,
1650*
*Nicolaas Stenius (1605-1670) is
one of the few Catholic priests
to be painted by Frans Hals. He
ministered to the town of*

*Akersloot and was a member of the
Haarlem chapter. Stenius regularly
attended meetings of the chapter
in Haarlem, and Hals may have
taken these as an opportunity to
paint his portrait.*

69
*Ciborium, Adam van Vianen,
Utrecht, 1615*
*Adam van Vianen, one of the
famous family of gold- and
silversmiths, manufactured
this ciborium for an unknown
hidden church. The ornate foot
features four winged angels'
heads showing various
emotions: smiling, laughing,
sleeping and crying. The heads
are interspersed by four Biblical
representations, encircled by so-
called auricular ornamentation.*

ministering to the town of Akersloot, Nicolaas Stenius (ill. 68) fell
into the hands of the bailiff after a raid on his place of worship.
Stenius came off well, however, probably because he paid the bailiff
handsomely: the bailiff received – albeit 'in utmost secrecy' – annual
payments of 3800 guilders for his tolerance of the practice of the
Roman Catholic faith in the villages of Kennemerland district.

There was also sufficient money for the decoration of these in-
house and hidden churches, which, while they could not permit
themselves any outward show, harboured beautiful works of art
inside (ill. 75). So it was that the well-known Utrecht-based gold and
silversmith Adam van Vianen was instructed to craft a pyx (ill. 69),
intended to hold the consecrated wafers. The monstrance made by
Michiel Esselbeeck in 1656 (ill. 70), decorated with medallions in
relief showing scenes relating to the sacrament, was used to display
the host in the hidden church of St Pancras in Castricum.

70

*Monstrance, Michiel Essel-
beeck, Amsterdam, 1656*
This monstrance for the display
of the consecrated host is highly
decorative with medallions in
relief referring to the Sacrament.
Depicted around the base are
seven saints of the Haarlem
diocese.

71

*Crucifixion, Abraham
Bloemaert, 1629*
In view of its generous
dimensions and upright format,
one can assume that this work
was an altar piece for an early
Catholic hidden church: Christ
on the cross between the two
thieves who were crucified
with Him. The darkened sky
symbolises the sin that is cast
out through the sacrifice of
Christ, whose body shines out
in a clear contrast with the
background.

72

Holy Family, Caesar van
Everdingen, around 1660
Mary, face on, holds up her child
for the viewer to see, while

Joseph, spectacles in hand, looks
out of the picture. Caesar van
Everdingen is held to belong to
the Haarlem classicists but

lived the best part of his life in
his home town of Alkmaar,
where he also died. The compo-
sition of the painting indicates it

was intended to be hung on
high, above a chimneypiece for
example.

Paintings indicate the major influence played by the important Roman Catholic council, the General Council of Trent (1546-1565). Here it was decreed, among other things, that in the depiction of the Crucifixion, Mary was no longer to be shown as swooning from grief (as occurs in Medieval paintings). The sacrifice on the Cross was after all a blessed event. As such the Utrecht artist Abraham Bloemaert (1629) (ill. 71) depicts Mary in dignified pose beneath the cross, in the company as always of Mary Magdalene and John the evangelist. The depiction of Joseph as an old man had also to change: henceforth he was to be shown as a man in the bloom of life. The fine painting by the Alkmaar painter Caesar van Everdingen (ill. 72) illustrates this transformation of the carpenter from Nazareth, while the work of the Utrecht artist Dirck van Baburen, *Coronation of thorns*, evokes sympathy because of its confrontational immediacy (ill. 73).

Tensions also arose within the Roman Catholic Church. Relations with Rome were strained; the Northern Netherlands were regarded as a missionary region. In addition differences in theological doctrine originated between different groups. A clear break occurred in 1723 when a number of priests re-invoked old rights and bypassed the authority of Rome to choose a new bishop for themselves. These 'old-Catholics' still exist today, forging their own choices independently of Rome.

73

Coronation of thorns, Dirck van Baburen, 1622/23

During a stay in Italy Dirck van Baburen became acquainted with the work of the Italian painter Caravaggio. This history piece depicts a scene from the Passion in a highly dramatic way. Through his use of life-sized upper-body figures and the tight cropping of the scene, this Utrecht 'Caravaggist' contrives to draw the viewer into the action.

74

74

*Communion ware, Johannes
du Vignon III, 1724*
This Holy Communion set
comes from the French Church
in Voorburg, founded by French
refugiés (refugees) who fled
France in fear of their lives
because of their Protestant
faith. Between 1680 and 1700
these refugees settled in the
Netherlands. For more than two
centuries the French Church in
Voorburg with its 200 seats
functioned as a place of worship
for the elite, as its sermons were
preached in French and the
serving 'pasteurs' or vicars,
were often particularly
eloquent.

75

*Chasuble, Amsterdam, second
quarter eighteenth century*
The church calendar determines
the colour of the chasuble, a
sleeveless vestment worn by the
priest when celebrating mass.
White is the colour required for
the celebration of feast days
such as Christmas and Easter.
The white silk of this festive
chasuble has been quilted
with embroidery in the form
of acanthus leaves and fruits.
The chasuble comes from the
clandestine church of Our Lord
in the Attic in Amsterdam.

The conflict within the Roman Catholic Church was further
intensified by the fact that in the early eighteenth century many
clerics with dissenting notions fled to the Netherlands from France.
They came to settle in a country that in earlier times had also
offered homes to refugees. In some cases such refugees were
individuals looking for freedom such as the French philosopher
René Descartes, for example, but often they came in large numbers,
like the Jews.

Alongside these refugees there were the French Protestants
who fled France in their thousands when the Edict of Nantes was
revoked in 1685. These 'Huguenots' joined the already existing
Walloon churches, set up by French-speaking refugees at the time
of the Revolt against Spain. In some rare cases the Huguenots set up
their own congregation, as happened in Voorburg, from which this
silverware for the celebration of Mass originates (ill. 74).

All these different groups coexisted in relative harmony. During
the course of the eighteenth century, the era of Enlightenment, new
ideas emerged, including new ways of looking at religion. Were not
all men equal, in principle? Was one church any better than another?
Eventually the National Meeting in 1796 decreed: 'A privileged
or dominant Church in the Netherlands can no longer and will no
longer be tolerated.'

Faith and Authority

Jeroen Koch
Tanja Kootte

76

Anniversary gift, given to
Abraham Kuyper to mark
the 25th anniversary of De
Standaard, J.M. van Kempen,
1897

Atop a black marble column
stands the Dutch virgin, holding
aloft a banner bearing the text
'Our help is in the name of the
Lord...'. She is flanked by the
Dutch lion. The two figures at
the base of the column represent
History and Religion. The
(Protestant) Anti-Revolutionary
Party (ARP) presented this
gift on the occasion of the
25th anniversary of the De
Standaard newspaper, of which
Kuyper was editor in chief.

The nineteenth century saw the final division between church and state. This enabled a Roman Catholic revival. Within the Protestant faith a series of new denominations sprang up. By the end of the nineteenth century, Protestants and Catholics, but also liberals and socialists had largely separated into discrete segregated communities (ill. 76). Each community of belief had its organisations in all walks of social life: politics, trade union, education, health services, media, youth movements and sport.

'All existing Religions will be granted equal protection; the professors of the same will enjoy the same civil rights and have equal claim to the exercise of merits, offices and services'. This was reasserted in the new constitution of 1814. With this the reformed church, henceforth known as the Dutch Reformed Church (Nederlandse Hervormde Kerk) definitively lost its special position as official public church. There was one comfort, however: 'The Christian reformed religion is that of the Sovereign monarch'. The king was held to be a member of the Dutch Reformed Church, a rule which still holds true today, although since 2004, the Reformed Church has been subsumed into the Protestantse Kerk Nederland (PKN, Protestant Church in the Netherlands).

The Reformed Church became the church of the established order with duties in education and ministration to the poor. Its theologians came from the ranks of the educated gentry. They were more distinguished, took on double-barrelled names and increasingly swapped the traditional coat and bands for the more chic gown. The Remonstrants had paved the way in this regard. Their preacher, Abraham des Amorie van der Hoeven, was a great advocate of this distinguished item of clothing and was portrayed posthumously wearing such a gown by painter Jan Adam Kruseman (ill. 77). Des Amorie was a leading orator from the pulpit who, although he was not reformed, was able to preach before King William II. And he sang in praise of God, the fatherland and the House of Orange, just as many of his peers expressed themselves in poetry at that time.

77
Abraham des Amorie van der Hoeven, J.A. Kruseman, 1855
Abraham des Amorie van der Hoeven (1798-1855) was a Remonstrant preacher in Rotterdam before becoming a lecturer at the Remonstrant Seminary in Amsterdam. Des Amorie is pictured in a toga, the church vestment of a preacher since the mid-nineteenth century.

The Netherlands was known as a protestant nation with an 'enlightened' or tolerant faith. But this 'enlightened' faith also prompted a reaction. New denominations and sects emerged in the nineteenth century, almost all as offshoots of the Reformed Church. Each new denomination felt itself to embody the 'true church' – that is to say, to go back to the community or church of the apostles.

The key reason behind this protestant fragmentation was that the Dutch Reformed Church did not instil a strict doctrinal discipline. Within the faith a great deal was possible. The official church authority, the synod, concerned itself exclusively with the 'external administration'. That led to dissatisfaction among the 'precisionists' or strictly orthodox, who wished to adhere strictly to the doctrine as determined by the synod of Dordrecht in 1618/19.

Challenged in their faith by newfangled liberal theology, the orthodox reformed rose up no less than three times against the power of the progressive ministers: during the aristocratic Reveil, during the populist Afscheiding (Schism) in 1834 (ill. 79) and in the Doelantie (Dissent) 1886, a union between the gentry and the lower middle classes under the leadership of Abraham Kuyper.

78

The raising of Jaïrus' daughter, Anthonius Brouwer, 1863
The Biblical story of the raising of Jaïrus' daughter from the dead (Mark 5:41) played a significant role in and after *1853. Among other things it was also depicted on medallions. In the story, Jesus says to the girl 'I say unto thee, arise'. The girl was not dead as everyone thought, but only sleeping.* *Jaïrus' daughter was likened to the Roman Catholic Church in the Netherlands, which had had no bishops since 1580. The appointment of five bishops in 1853 ended this state of affairs* *and emphasised that the Catholic Church in the Netherlands was vital and alive.*

K.C.Verlaan

*Religious service of a
breakaway congregation in
a Gelderland farmer's home,
J. Verlaan, circa 1910*
In 1834 orthodox Protestants
under the leadership of parson
Hendrick de Cock broke away
from the Reformed Church. They
fell victim to persecution, for the
government viewed division
within the church as a danger
to Dutch unity. In barns and
in private homes they came
together for their services of
worship.

Faith and Authority

Christianity in the Netherlands

80

Devotional cabinet with
crucifix, F.W. Mengelberg,
J.H. Brom, C. Lindsen, 1880
This diminutive cabinet,
executed in the neo-gothic style,
was a gift to Adriaan Ariëns to
mark his silver anniversary as
chairman of the Roman Catholic
poor relief in Utrecht. Adriaan
was father to Alphons Ariëns,
the priest who in 1889 founded
the Netherlands' first Catholic
labour union, in Enschede.

81
Detail of a stained glass
window, O. Mengelberg, 1917
This fragment comes from a
glass window in the Our Lady
of the Ascension Church in
Utrecht's Biltstraat. This neo-
gothic building, built in 1893/94
to a design by Alfred Tepe, was
demolished in 1972. Much was
lost, with only some fragments
of the glass windows able to be
saved.

These church rebellions partly explain the rich diversity of denominations. Most originated in pietistic circles, where the experience of
God was considered more important than church orthodoxy. After
1848, when the new, liberal constitution reaffirmed the division
between church and state, the state no longer busied itself with such
church upheavals unless they posed a threat to public order.

The Netherlands was also a protestant nation in the eyes of the
liberals, the majority of whom were freethinking Protestants.
Constitution in hand, they set about reorganising the country. As
a consequence of the revised constitution of 1848 the division
between church and state became absolute, thereby paving the way
for the reinstatement of the Roman Catholic episcopal hierarchy
(1853). The Pope's decision to do so, however, raised a storm of
protest. Did it not mark the beginning of the end for the Protestant
nation state? This was indeed the view of the Protestants who
united under the banner of the so-called April Movement. Fruitlessly
they attempted to thwart the new religious order.

Roman Catholics compared the revival of their church with the
Biblical story of Jairus' daughter. Just as Jesus raised her from the
dead (ill. 78), so the Roman Catholic church was now woken from
its centuries of 'sleep'.

82

Chalice, J.H. Brom, 1909
This beautiful golden chalice
was made by the Utrecht gold-
smith Jan Hendrik Brom (1860-
1915)
The chalice is modelled on its
medieval equivalent and is
decorated with enamels and
88 coloured stones, among other
things. The commission came
from a rich cattle farmer who,
according to the inscription on
the base, ordered it made for his
grandson Peter van den Burg on
his ordination as priest.

Religious plate

Magnificent chalices and other liturgical plate were
made by the Utrecht-based silversmith Brom (ill. 82).
Father Gerard Bartel Brom founded the workshop in
1856 and during the era of Catholic emancipation
specialised in neo-gothic ware. Son Jan Hendrik
Brom abandoned the neo-gothic in favour of modern
design. The brothers Jan Eloy and Leo, together with
sister Joanna and Jan Eloy's wife Hildegard, grew
the business into a leading workshop for modern
liturgical ware. But did such pomp and circumstance
belong in the church? In 1961 the workshop closed,
not only because of the lack of successors to take it
over, but also because the demand for church silver
had declined dramatically.

83

Gold brocade chasuble,
Dutch?, nineteenth century
On the rear of the garment a
richly decorated cross in heavy
gold and some silver thread has
been embroidered onto the gold
brocade. The centre of the cross
bears the letters IHS, which
stand for Jesus' name. This
chasuble comes from the
Monastery of the Missionaries
of the Holy Heart in Brummen.

84

Madonna wreathed in flowers,
Belgium, around 1875
From the late nineteenth century
it became popular among
Catholics to place images of
Mary, Joseph and the Christ
Child in their homes. Workshops
manufactured such images in
large numbers, modelling them
from china, porcelain or plaster.
The statuettes were most often
painted in pastel tints. The
flowers are made from textile
scraps. A bell jar protects this
particular devotional image
from dust.

From 1860 onwards the Roman Catholics built a string of magnificent churches whose towering steeples dominated town and countryside. The architectural style they opted for was neo-gothic, which eventually was to become a typically Catholic style (ill. 80). The style harked back to the gothic architecture of the Middle Ages, which they viewed as the highpoint of Christian culture. The leading architects of this style included Pierre Cuypers and Alfred Tepe. The imposing stained glass windows (ill. 81) of the Church of Our Lady built by Tepe in the Biltstraat in Utrecht were made by Otto Mengelberg (1867-1924).

But however bitter the enmity between Protestant and Catholic, the education policy pursued by the liberals forced them into a holy

85

Girl at prayer, J.Th. Toorop,
1927

With a devout expression on her
face and a cross clasped tightly
to her breast, a girl kneeling
before an altar meditates on
the suffering of Christ. On the
wall hangs a painting depicting
His fall from the cross. This
representation was highly
popular for a long time and
was often used in miniature as
a devotional print in prayer
books.

alliance. The schools conflict, which wrestled with the question of whether state schools and faith-based schools should be put on an equal financial footing, put religion at the centre of the political arena. In a society that embraced freedom of religion and association, this prompted a movement that was to result in the far-reaching compartmentalisation of Dutch society along religious lines, the so-called 'verzuiling' (pillarization).

The schools conflict centred on matters of principle. Which could lay claim to ultimate loyalty, the authority of the church or the authority of the state? To what extent was the state entitled to intervene in the personal domain, which the liberals in particular had always ordained was where religion belonged? Who were the true Dutch? Did the Catholics, loyal as they were to the Pope, truly, fully belong? Had the Eighty Years War not been a battle for the true religion and consequently weren't orthodox Protestants – guardians of the 'faith of the fathers' – better Dutchmen than the liberals? It was only when the Second World War broke out that a new enemy emerged, unifying the Dutch into a nation of equals.

In all the European countries where the state elbowed the church out of education a similar conflict ensued. But only in the Netherlands did it result in 'verzuiling': the compartmentalisation of politics and society along religious and ideological lines. Carefully and methodically the different emancipated communities constructed their own ideological cells.

Right up until 1960 the influence of organised religion remained large and obvious – in church architecture, processions, flag-waving by social and political organisations and schools 'with the Bible'. This religious enthusiasm enjoyed broad support. Monasteries blossomed and missionaries and proselytisers spread the word of Christ. A mass church culture (ill. 83, 84, 85) developed alongside, with innumerable religious objects positioned somewhere between art and kitsch. Therese were not always objects of superior artistic quality. But this religious kitsch serves to show just how faith permeated all aspects of life, both in the Protestant and in the Catholic community. Mary even made her appearance onto biscuit tins.

7

Liberation and Reflection

Joost de Wal

*The second half of the twentieth century was an era of turbulent change in
Dutch Christianity. The period is characterised by shrinking congregations,
secularisation and church decline but also by a new religious élan. While
church and tradition continue to exist, the ways in which the Christian
message is embraced become increasingly free and individualistic. Society
loses its compartmentalisation along religious lines and increasingly takes
on a multicultural, multi-religious character. The visual arts form part of all
these developments, but at the same time represent a lively reflection of them.*

The situation within Dutch Christianity in the first half of
the twentieth century is little different from that in the late
nineteenth century. Catholics and Protestants pursue their
emancipation and the compartmentalisation of Dutch society along
religious lines becomes increasingly entrenched. But in contrast
with earlier centuries, art seldom serves directly to 'illustrate' the
developments in church and society. This reporting and recording
function is taken over by photography, film and later television.
Visual art becomes autonomous, develops along its own lines and
encounters its own problems. At the same time, however, it is a myth
that modern art no longer has any ties to religion.

In earlier times art that took a Christian subject as its theme was
almost automatically suited for display in a church building or
space within the religious domain. But in the twentieth century the
difference between art commissioned by the church in the Netherlands and free Christian work executed independently of the church
became greater and greater. The Roman Catholic Church retained a
preference for artistic styles from the past, such as the neo-Gothic
and neo-Roman. By way of contrast free Christian art sought to ally
itself with new trends in modern art. Some artists found themselves
able to straddle the two worlds, artists like Otto van Rees (1884-1957)
and Matthieu Wiegman (1886-1971). However, art that was too
modern was not appreciated. Immediately after the Second World

87

Saint Willibrord, Dolf Henkes,
1939
The archbishop of the Frisians
wears a monk's habit and on
his chest a cross. He can be
recognised by the stone jug,
mitre and bishop's staff. The
painting was made to mark the
1200 year commemoration of
Willibrord's death.

War, for example, Aad de Haas (1920-1972) was commissioned by the parish to paint the Stations of the Cross in the tiny church of Wahlwiller in the province of Limburg. Not long after its completion, however, in 1949 his unorthodox rendition – Mary sports a hat and Mary Magdalene carries an umbrella – was removed at the behest of the Holy See (the Vatican). It was only in 1981 that they were restored, this time as protected items of cultural heritage.

One of De Haas' major influences, the Rotterdam-based painter Dolf Henkes (1903-1989) was among the first to adopt a rough and expressive style of painting. Prior to the Second World War this style was certainly far from usual in the portrayal of sacred subjects. Henkes grew up as a working class Catholic lad in the Rotterdam harbour area. He was deeply committed to his faith, but consistently adopted an irreverent approach. A painting such as *Sint Willibrord* (ill. 87) offers an example of how he quirkily reinterpreted well-known Christian themes without discarding tradition, as shown here by his use of attributes and symbols (the stone jug and bishop's staff). Henkes' work inspired post-war artists to further explore the boundaries of Christian art.

88

Piëta, Ossip Zadkine, 1955
The Piëta (It. pietà, meaning
pity) is one of the great motifs
of suffering in Christian art:
Mary bewails her dead son,
who lies on her lap. In this
statue parts of the figures have
been omitted or misshapen in
a cubist manner, which further
serves to intensify the sense
of pain and suffering. In the
Netherlands Zadkine is famous
principally for his war memorial
The ravaged city/City
without a heart in Rotterdam
in 1953. Inevitably his Pietà
also refers to the suffering of
the Second World War.

89

Blue Madonna, Jacques
Frenken, around 1965
Frenken re-used the plaster
images the churches discarded
after the Second Vatican Council
– in a process dubbed by some
'the second iconoclastic fury'.
Frenken sawed up statues of
Mary, mounted a plaster
Christ on a target or, in The
Temptation of Anthony,
mounted molten dolls' heads
alongside a representation of
the saint. In this way familiar
religious images took on a new
religious meaning. Some
believers saw Frenken as the
antichrist, others found his
work liberating and wanted to
order smaller exemplars for
themselves. Since then Frenken's
sacred pop art has become an
icon of Sixties Dutch society.

The horrors of the Second World War had a profound impact on
Dutch society. Initially they forged unity and brotherly love among
the churches. The beginning of the post-war reconstruction of the
Netherlands was accompanied by a strong desire for innovation and
ecumenism. Even so it was not long before the various groupings
retreated back into their own segregated worlds once more. In the
'world after Auschwitz' the *Piëta* of the Russian-French sculptor
Ossip Zadkine (1890-1967) would indubitably have evoked strong
emotions – as indeed it does today (ill. 88). Zadkine renders the
suffering of Christ by omitting parts of His broken body and by
emphasising its gauntness. The image of Christ in modern art is
often that of His suffering; in terms of its expression Zadkine's Piëta,
which stylistically follows from Cubism, reaches back to the tragic
pietàs of the late Middle Ages.

The early 1950s were years of hard work, calm and respect for authority. Church and faith represented an important source of stability. But as standards of living improved, so did individualism and people's wish to have more say. This was reflected in an increasing resistance to authority and institutions. The Episcopal Charge of 1954, aimed at bolstering unity among Catholics – among other things, Catholics were forbidden to become members of socialist groupings – but it could not turn the tide of a more open, desegregated Catholicism. Among Protestants, too, there was more room for openness and contemporary ideas, such as the theology of the Swiss professor Karl Barth.

The Second Vatican Council (1962-1965) signified a major innovative impulse from Rome. The Council concentrated on *aggiornamento*, bringing the Church up to date. In the Netherlands, this had a major impact on the liturgy and church furnishings and decor. Out of a desire for a greater austerity that coincided with ongoing secularisation, shrinking congregations and church demolition, many cheap neo-gothic plaster statues were removed from church buildings. Some were subsequently taken by the Den Bosch-based artist Jacques Frenken (born 1929) to his studio, where he sawed them up and painted them. In this way Frenken, who at one time aspired to the priesthood and studied at a seminary for several years, created *Blue Madonna* (around 1965): a series of almost identical Mary figures that disappear into one another, creating a Chinese box effect (ill. 89). Frenken's sacred pop art prompted a storm of protest in some quarters and enthusiastic endorsement in others. Meanwhile the devotional statues of plaster to be found in so many Dutch households were also being discarded as sentimental

90

Untitled, Reinoud van Vught, 1991

Van Vught found a new use for the discarded devotional objects he found in his studio in a monastery attic: he pressed the crucifixes deep into a thick layer of paint and then pulled them free. His radical methods meant the statues often broke – sometimes they even remained embedded in the paint. In this way a new way of representing the Crucifixion emerged, in which Christ leaves His traces and the meditation on suffering flows into the material.

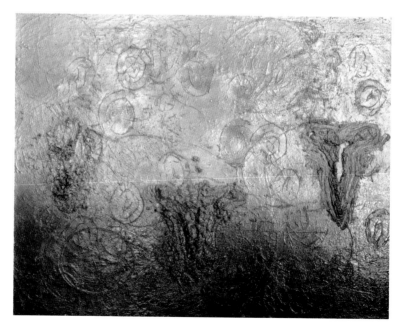

91
*Mohair habit, Aziz, winter
2000/2001 collection*
The Amsterdam fashion
designer Aziz designed a habit
as everyday wear. This gown
is reminiscent of the clothing
of some Christian as well as
Islamic priests. Aziz designed a
similar garment in purple and
black for the role of the high
priest Zacharias in Verdi's
Nabucco opera; just like the
habit it has major sculptural
power.

92
*Number Two (Just because I'm
standing here doesn't mean I
want to), Guido van der
Werve, 2003*
Van der Werve's video
presentations often deal with
absurd, alienating moments in
our own familiar world. In
Number Two the shock of the
unexpected death is followed by
a remarkable apotheosis: angel-
like dancers step out from the
back of the riot police van and
execute a consolatory heavenly
ballet. In the visual arts – of
which video and dvd art have
become a part – life's big
questions are no longer
automatically afforded a
Christian answer, but are
worked out in a probing,
existential manner.

kitsch. From the Sixties onwards, but particularly in the 1980s and
1990s, such statues were frequently re-used in art. Joost van den
Toorn (born 1954) converted a plaster statue of the Virgin Mary into
a symbolic St Hubert, the early Christian martyr who converted to
Christianity during the hunt, when an image of the Crucifix
appeared between the antlers of the stag he was pursuing (ill. 86).

Reinoud van Vught (born 1960) pressed the crucifixes he found in
his studio in the attic of a former monastery deep into the paint: the

93

The Stairway at St. Paul's,
Jeroen Offerman, 2002
Stood in front of London's St
Paul's Cathedral, the artist sings
the rock classic Stairway to
Heaven (1970) by Led Zeppelin.
The song text has been learned
backwards, and the film
subsequently played backwards.
Like a latter day troubadour,
Offerman preaches a timeless,
personal message in a hectic
society.

result was a new and meaningful variation on the age-old rendition of Golgotha (ill. 90). By this time the post-modern actions of artists such as Van den Toorn and Van Vught no longer prompted any protest.

The continuing process of decompartmentalisation and secularisation by no means signified the end of religion. Since the 1980s there has been a renewed interest in the Christian foundation of western culture. However this trend has gone hand in hand with a further decline of the church as institution and authority. Multiculturalism is on the increase, and with it religious plurality. A broad interest exists in spiritual tendencies and a clearer manifestaion of religions such as Islam and Judaism. These tendencies have also found their way into the visual arts. The habit designed by Aziz (Aziz Bekkaoui, born 1969) has not been conceived of as a religious robe, but does closely resemble the clothes of some priests (ill. 91). Here the profane shades over into the sacred and both traditions serve as an example to one another. Video art broadly explores major ontological questions. In Guido van der Werve's (born 1977) video, death is mourned in a poignant and heavenly ballet (ill. 92). The video made by Jeroen Offerman (born 1970) is more than merely an innovative 'trick' that makes optimal use of the possibilities offered by the medium: it represents the age-old image of the street singer performing his own personal 'stairway to heaven' before the steps of the cathedral (ill. 93). And even within church art new objects have emerged for the liturgy. The altar ware of the artist Ruudt Peters (born 1950) little resembles the holy pomp of bygone eras (ill. 94). The strength of the work emanates from its incorporation of new materials, poignant use of image and its rich emotional associations with Holy Communion and the sacrament. It is one of the many faces of Dutch Christianity within the multi-faceted world of faith and religion.

94

Liturgical plate: chalice and wafer dish, Ruudt Peters, 2004

Peters designed a 50-piece service for the chapel of Amsterdam's VU University Medical Center. A number of pieces were duplicated for the Catharijneconvent Museum. Each piece is based on two forms that mirror one another and are connected to one another by a textile layer. The textile is covered in red (Communion) and transparent (baptism) plastic. The section that has been cut away is both functional (it allows for a good grip) and symbolic (a reference to Christ's wounds).

Europe and the Holy Land

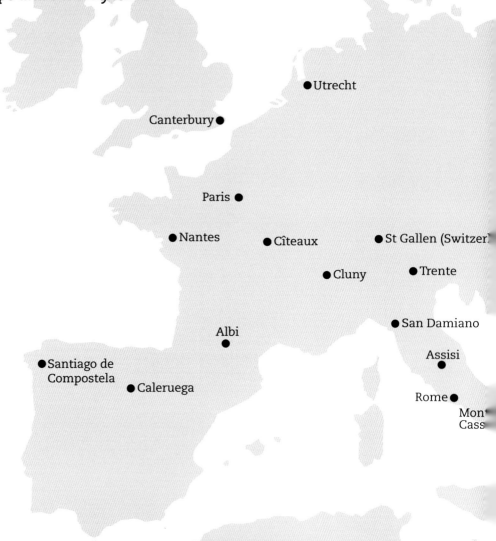

●Utrecht

Canterbury●

Paris ●

●Nantes   ●Cîteaux   ●St Gallen (Switzerl

●Cluny   ●Trente

●San Damiano

Albi   Assisi
●   ●

●Santiago de   Rome●
Compostela
●Caleruega   Mon
Cass

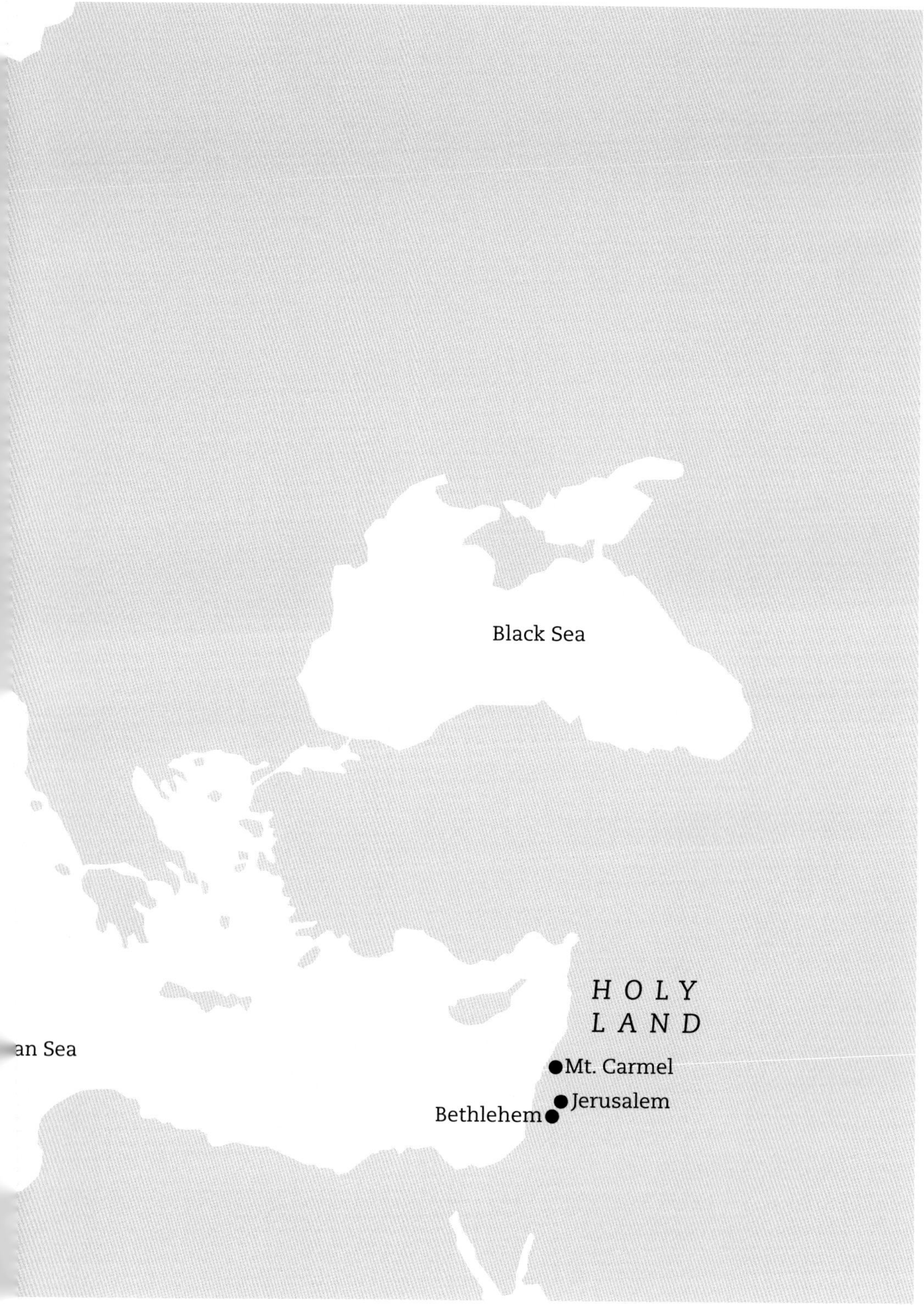

Black Sea

HOLY
LAND

an Sea

●Mt. Carmel
●Jerusalem
Bethlehem●

The Netherlands

(The dotted line indicates the current border)

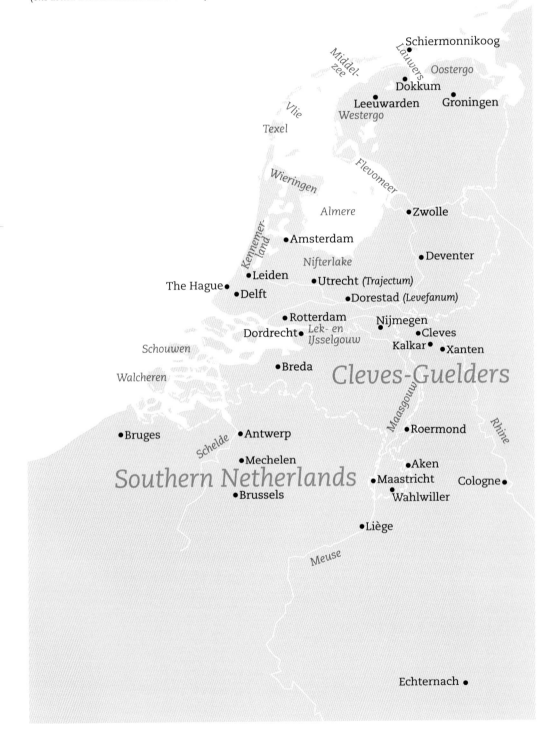

Schiermonnikoog

Middel-
zee

Lauwers

Oostergo

Dokkum

Vlie

Leeuwarden

Groningen

Texel

Westergo

Flevomeer

Wieringen

Almere

Zwolle

Kennemer-
land

Amsterdam

Deventer

Nifterlake

Leiden

Utrecht *(Trajectum)*

The Hague

Delft

Dorestad *(Levefanum)*

Rotterdam

Nijmegen

Dordrecht

Lek- en
IJsselgouw

Cleves

Kalkar

Xanten

Schouwen

Breda

Cleves-Guelders

Walcheren

Maasgouw

Rhine

Bruges

Antwerp

Roermond

Schelde

Mechelen

Southern Netherlands

Aken

Maastricht

Cologne

Brussels

Wahlwiller

Liège

Meuse

Echternach

Glossary

Abbess – the head and administrator of a convent.

Abbot – the head and administrator of a monastery.

Alb – a long, white linen vestment worn by the priest and his assistants under the outer-garment during Mass and other services.

Altar – a table, generally of stone, on which Communion is celebrated. From the early Middle Ages onwards the altar would hold relics.

Apostle – one who preaches the gospel. Often used to refer to one of the twelve disciples originally chosen by Christ.

Archbishop – the most important bishop of the church province.

Archbishopric – the most important diocese in a church province. A church province consists of a number of dioceses.

Ascetic – one who attempts to cleanse himself of sin through fasting and prayer.

Asceticism – the exercise of actions such as fasting and prayer for the good of the soul.

Bishop – ecclesiastical leader of a diocese. Alongside the powers of the priesthood, ordination as a bishop confers the right to ordinate priests and consecrate churches and altars. The bishop is further entrusted with the task of governing the bishopric. The ornaments of office are a ring, mitre and staff, which are worn during the liturgy.

Bishopric – also known as a diocese. The area governed by a bishop. In late Antiquity bishoprics coincided with the old Roman provinces or *civitates*.

Cathedral – the principal church of a diocese, or bishop's church. The place where the bishop presides and his *cathedra* (seat or throne) is situated. Utrecht is the only city in the Netherlands to have a cathedral, known in Dutch as the 'Domkerk' or 'Dom'.

Chapter – a community of canons linked to a church.

Ciborium – also known as a pyx. This was a consecrated gilded or golden cup-shaped vessel lid for holding the consecrated host.

Cleric – member of the clergy.

Communion – the act of receiving consecrated bread and sometimes also wine at the Mass.

Confession – one of the seven sacraments of the Roman Catholic Church. A rite in which an inividual confesses his or her sins to a priest, followed by absolution.

Consecration – Roman Catholic ritual of the ceremonial blessing of bread and wine by a priest at Mass. According to Roman Catholic doctrine the bread and wine are transformed into the body and blood of Christ during this ritual.

Contact relic – object that has been in contact with the body of a saint during his or her life or after death.

Cope – wide cloak or robe worn by priests during special ceremonies.

Copyist – someone who copies manuscripts, also known as a scribe or transcriptor.

Council – church meeting.

Eucharist – (Greek: thanksgiving) the principal sacrament of the Roman Catholic Church, also known as Mass, Lord's Supper or Holy Communion. The ritual in which bread and wine are consecrated, while recalling the words that Jesus Christ uttered during the Last Supper.

Gospel – the teachings of Jesus Christ. The word is also used to indicate one of the four books in the New Testament recounting the life of Jesus, attributed to the Evangelists Matthew, Mark, Luke and John.

Gothic – artistic style dating from the late Middle Ages which is characterized by geometric uniformity, airiness, allowing a great deal of light to enter the church and by a drive for the vertical; one built upwards, towards God.

Hadj – Islamic pilgrimage to Mecca.

Hierarchy – ranking of those ordained for religious service. In the Roman Catholic Church these were: the pope, bishops, priests, deacons, subdeacons and the lower orders.

Holy Sacrament – synonym for the Eucharist.

Host – (literally: sacrifice) the large wafer of bread that is consecrated by the priest during Mass.

Hours – the daily round of prayer consisting of the services Matins, Lauds, Prime, Terce, Sext, Nones, Vespers and Compline, which are celebrated at a fixed time of day.

Indulgence – a partial exoneration of the temporal punishment a sinner had to undergo in purgatory. It was often granted in return for a sum of money.

Martyr – a Christian tortured and murdered for his or her faith

Mass – Roman Catholic celebration of the Eucharist preceded by the liturgy of the Word (previously known as the pre-Mass) with prayers from amongst others the Gospels, followed by the consecration of bread and wine and Communion and finally the closing prayers and concluding blessing.

Mission – preaching of the faith by Roman Catholics or proselytizing by Protestants.

Missionary – priest actively dedicated to spreading the faith.

Monastery – a community of monks who segregate themselves from the world in order to dedicate themselves to God who live under a rule. Unlike a hermit, the monks live together in a community. Nuns coexisting in such communities live together in **convents**.

Monk – a man who has entered the monastery and has taken the monastic vows (usually poverty, chastity and obedience).

Monstrance – a gold or gilded silver receptacle in which the consecrated host can be put on display.

Neo-gothic – style from the nineteenth and early twentieth century inspired by Gothic.

Nun – woman who has entered a convent and has taken the **monastic** vows (usually poverty, chastity and obedience).

Patron saint – a saint of whom a group or community (a city, monastery, or guild, or people suffering from a certain type of illness) expect special help or protection.

Penance – to do penance is to undergo a punishment, often prescribed by a priest, for one's sins. Pilgrimages were seen as a form of penance.

Perigrinatio (pro deo) – literally 'wandering for God'. The idea behind the perigrinatio tradition is to leave one's safe and familiar fatherland to give oneself up entirely to the will of God.

Pietism – current within Dutch Protestantism which emphasizes deep personal devotional feeling.

Pilgrim – a believer who embarks on a journey to a holy place or place of pilgrimage, for the good of his soul.

Pope – the bishop of Rome and successor to the apostle Peter. During the course of the Middle Ages he established himself as the head of the Roman Catholic Church.

Priest – a cleric who has been ordained to the priesthood and is therefore authorised to conduct the sacraments of penance and absolution, Eucharist, baptism, the anointing of the sick and marriage.

Procession – ceremonial march or circumambulation of priests and congregation in and/or outside the church walls.

Purgatory – place where the deceased suffer temporary punishment for their sins before being allowed into Heaven.

Relic – remains (Latin: *reliquiae*) of a saint, generally a part of the body (for example a nail, or fingertip) or a piece of clothing (an object that has been in contact with the saint).

Reliquary – decorative box, cross or other container in which relics were kept.

Sacraments – (Roman Catholic) holy acts which can only be undertaken by a priest or bishop and which offer mercy. The Roman Catholic Church numbers seven sacraments: baptism, confirmation, the Eucharist, penance and absolution, anointing of the sick, the ordination of priests and marriage.

(Protestant) holy acts in which expression is given to the unity with God. Most Protestant churches recognise two sacraments – baptism and communion.

Saint – a holy man or woman who has excelled in piety and good deeds and of whom the Roman Catholic Church has officially decreed by canonization.

Scapular – a band of some thirty centimetres in width with a collar in its centre, worn over the breast and back and generally a little shorter than the cassock underneath.

Synod – church meeting

Bibliography

Acquoy, J.G.R., *Het klooster te Windesheim en zijn invloed*, Amsterdam 1968, 3 vols. in 2 bnd. (orig. pub. Utrecht 1875-1880, 3 vols.)

Angenendt, A., *Das Frühmittelalter. Die abendländische Christenheit von 400 bis 900*, Stuttgart (etc.) 1990

Bank, J. and M. van Buuren, *1900. Hoogtij van de burgerlijke cultuur*, Den Haag 2000 (Nederlandse cultuur in Europese context)

Bertrand, C., Aad de Haas, *De schilderingen en kruiswegstaties in de Sint-Cunibertuskerk te Wahlwiller*, 2e dr., Nuth 1998

Blom, J.H.C. and J. Talsma (ed.), *De verzuiling voorbij. Godsdienst, stand en natie in de lange negentiende eeuw*, Amsterdam 2000

Bos, D., *In dienst van het Koninkrijk. Beroepsontwikkeling van hervormde predikanten in negentiende-eeuws Nederland*, Amsterdam 1999

Bouma, G., P. van de Laar and R. Vroegindeweij, *Dolf Henkes (1903-1989). Eigenzinnig en ongrijpbaar*, Schiedam 2003

Clemens, T., W. Otten and G. Rouwhorst (ed.), *Het einde nabij? Toekomstverwachting en angst voor het oordeel in de geschiedenis van het christendom*, Nijmegen 1999

Deursen, A.Th. van, *De last van veel geluk. De geschiedenis van Nederland 1555-1702*, Amsterdam 2004

Eijnatten, J. van and F. van Lieburg, *Nederlandse religiegeschiedenis*, Hilversum 2005

Frijhoff, W. and M. Spies, *1650. Bevochten eendracht*, Den Haag 1999

Goddijn, W., J. Jacobs and G. van Tillo (ed.), *Tot vrijheid geroepen. Katholieken in Nederland: 1946-2000*, Baarn 1999

Goudriaan, K., 'De derde orde van Sint-Franciscus in het bisdom Utrecht. Een voorstudie', in: *Jaarboek voor middeleeuwse geschiedenis* 1 (1998), p. 205-260

Goudriaan, K., 'Boekdistributie langs kerkelijke kanalen in de late Middeleeuwen', in: *Jaarboek voor Nederlandse boekgeschiedenis* 8 (2001), p. 43-58

Klaasen, G. (collected), *Aanzien kerk en godsdienst in Nederland en België, 1945-1985*, Utrecht/Antwerpen 1985

Knippenberg, H., *De religieuze kaart van Nederland. Omvang en geografische spreiding van de godsdienstige gezindten vanaf de Reformatie tot heden*, Assen (etc.) 1992

Moll, W., *Kerkgeschiedenis van Nederland voor de hervorming*, vol. II.2, Arnhem 1867

Mostert, M., *754: Bonifatius bij Dokkum vermoord*, Hilversum 1999 (Verloren verleden. Gedenkwaardige momenten en figuren uit de vaderlandse geschiedenis, 7)

Otten, W., 'The power of the bible in the Middle Ages', in: W.R. Farmer (ed.), *The international bible commentary*, Collegeville 1998, p. 48-52

Padberg, L. von, *Mission und Christianisierung: Formen und Folgen bei Angelsachsen und Franken in 7. und 8. Jahrhundert*, Stuttgart 1995

Pijfers, H. and J. Roes, *Memoriale. Katholiek leven in Nederland in de twintigste eeuw*, Zwolle 1996

Pranger, M.B., *Bernard of Clairvaux and the shape of monastic thought. Broken dreams*, Leiden 1994

Rogier, J.L., *Katholieke herleving. Geschiedenis van katholiek Nederland sinds 1853*, 2nd ed., Den Haag 1956

Rooden, P. van, *Religieuze regimes in Nederland. Over godsdienst en maatschappij in Nederland, 1570-1990*, Amsterdam 1996

Steensma, R. (ed.), *Jezus is boos. Het beeld van Christus in de hedendaagse kunst*, Zoetermeer 1995 (Religie en kunst, 2)

Struick, J.E.A.L., *Utrecht door de eeuwen heen*, Utrecht/Antwerpen 1968

Valk, J.P. de, *Roomser dan de paus? Studies over de betrekkingen tussen de Heilige Stoel en het Nederlandse katholicisme 1815–1940*, Nijmegen 1998 (KDC Bronnen & studies, 36)

Vlierden, M. van, *Willibrord en het begin van Nederland*, Utrecht 1995 (Clavis kunsthistorische monografieën, 15)

Wal, J. de, *Kunst zonder kerk. Nederlandse beeldende kunst en religie, 1945-1990*, Amsterdam 2002

Wüstefeld, W.C.M., *Middeleeuwse boeken van het Catharijneconvent*, Utrecht/Zwolle 1993

Illustrated works

Cover: detail of ill.60, ill.86
Inside cover front: see ill.94
Inside cover back: see ill.11
Frontispiece: Marc Mulders, *Apocalypse*
StCC v142

1 Hammer belonging to St Martin
   OKM m38
2 Utrecht, *Shield for cope depicting the
   ordination of Willibrord* ABM t2077
3 *Fragment of the alb belonging to
   Odulphus* OKM st86a
4 *Merovingian reliquary* ABM m904
5 Palace School at Aachen, *Lebuinus'
   chalice* ABM bi787
6 Northern France / Cologne, *Lebuinus
   codex* ABM h1
7 Northern France / Cologne, *Lebuinus
   codex: beginning of the Gospel of St
   Luke* ABM h1 , f. 69r
8 St Gallen, *Ansfridus codex* ABM h2
9 Maasland, *Procession crucifix*
   ABM m1028
10 Northern Netherlands, *Holy monk*
   BMH bh227
11 Reichenau, *Bernulphus codex* ABM h3
12 Reichenau, *Bernulphus codex:
   evangelist St Mark* ABM h3, f. IV
13 Utrecht, *Francis of Assisi* ABM bh599
14 Northern Netherlands, *Clara*
   BMH bh307
15 Utrecht, *Mary with child appearing to
   St Dominic in a vision* ABM s71
16 Henrick Douwerman, *St Christopher*
   ABM bh251
17 Southern Germany, *Pilgrim saint*
   ABM bh621
18 Canterbury, *Pilgrim's ampoule showing Thomas Becket and two knights*
   RMCC m448
19 Limoges, *Reliquary of Thomas Becket*
   ABM m907
20 Cologne, *Reliquary bust of one of
   Ursula's companions* RMCC b72
21 Utrecht, *Ursula and her travelling
   companions* ABM bh252
22 Bethlehem, *Model of the Church of
   the Holy Sepulchre in Jerusalem*
   BMH v1575a
23 Constantinople, *Mother of God
   Hodegetria* ABM bi751
24 *Catharijneconvent, view of the south
   wing*
25 Amsterdam, *Church of the Nativity in
   Bethlehem with four Jerusalem pilgrims*
   ABM s104
26 Geertgen tot Sint-Jans, *Christ as Man
   of Suffering* ABM s63
27 Antwerp, *Mourning woman featured
   in a representation of the Passion*
   RMCC b109
28 Utrecht, *Commemorative panel showing Christ on the cross, saints and
   kneeling founders* ABM s194
29 Master of the bible from Zwolle,
   *Initial showing Bernard hugging the
   cross* ABM h111
30 Adriaen van Wesel, *Holy family in
   the carpenter's workshop* ABM bh471

31 Delft, *Book of Hours: Annunciation*
   ABM h20, f. 82v-83r
32 Mechelen, *Seated Christ Child* RMCC
   b194
33 Arnt van Kalkar and Zwolle, *Apostle
   Paul* ABM bh493
34 Northern France or Flanders, *Diptych showing scenes from the life of
   Christ* ABM bi754
35 Worms?, *Gethsemane group* ABM
   bh567-570
36 Brussels?, *Veronica and the grieving
   women beneath the cross* SMCC b1
   and SMCC b2
37 Master of the Spring of Life,
   Gregorian mass RMCC s194
38 Northern Netherlands, *Shield on the
   cope of David of Burgundy* OKM t89
39 Master of the Utrecht Woman's
   Head in Stone *Head and shoulders of
   a Mary figure* ABM bs604
40 Maasland, *Mary with child* ABM
   bh261
41 Mechelen, *'Anna-te-drieën'* (St Anne
   with Mary and the infant Jesus)
   ABM bh348
42 Northern Netherlands, *Mary on the
   grassy bank* ABM s65
43 Middle Rhine region, *Annunciation*
   ABM s25.01
44 Delft, *Breviary belonging to Beatrijs of
   Assendelft* OKM h3, f. 166v
45 Copy after Quinten Matsijs,
   Desiderius Erasmus RMCC s80
46 Southern Netherlands, *Tabernacle*
   ABM bs641
47 Antwerp, *Crook of the bishop's staff
   belonging to Aegidius de Monte*
   OKM m161
48 Jacob Cornelisz. van Oostsanen,
   *Abraham surveys the devastation of
   Sodom* RMCC v584
49 Lucas Cranach, *Martin Luther*
   RMCC s107
50 Northern Netherlands, *Parable of
   the Good Shepherd* StCC s47
51 Netherlands, *Weighing scales of the
   true religion* SPKK s24
52 Netherlands?, *Satirical cartoon mocking the Pope* BMH s56
53 Jacob van Liesvelt (ed.), *The so-called
   Liesvelt Bible* BMH Warm pi1259F8,
   f. ciii
54 Kleef-Gelre, *Head of a Christ figure*
   ABM bs708
55 Dirck van Delen, *Allegory on the
   tyranny of Alva* RMCC s91
56 Maarten de Vos, *Moses with the
   tablets, encircled by two families*
   RMCC s94
57 Pieter Saenredam, *Interior of the
   Grote Kerk in Alkmaar* BMH s124
58 Northern Netherlands, *Peace exhorts
   the churches to be tolerant* RMCC s48
59. David Micheel, *Baptismal charger
   from the Reformed Church in Bergen*
   SPKK m180
60 Gijsbert Sibilla *Interior of the Grote
   Kerk or Laurentius Church in Weesp*
   RMCC s88
61 Northern Netherlands, *Family saying
   grace before the meal* RMCC s49

62 Northern Netherlands, *Majolica plate*
   RMCC v724
63 Rembrandt van Rijn, *Baptism of the
   Eunuch* ABM s380
64 Ferdinand Bol, *Gideon's sacrifice*
   RMCC s24
65 Pieter Fransz. de Grebber, *A penitent
   David chooses between three plagues*
   StCC s28
66 Wed. J. van Someren (ed.), *States
   Bible* RMCC od21
67 Essaias van de Velde, *Arminian Muck
   Wagon* StCC s48
68 Frans Hals, *Nicolaas Stenius*
   BMH s662
69 Adam van Vianen, *Ciborium*
   ABM m1248
70 Michiel Esselbeeck, *Monstrance*
   BMH m10050
71 Abraham Bloemaert, *Crucifixion*
   BMH s3869
72 Caesar van Everdingen, *Holy Family*
   BMH s115
73 Dirck van Baburen, *Coronation of
   thorns* StCC s9
74 Johannes du Vignon III, *Communion
   ware* RMCC m28a,b
75 Amsterdam, *Chasuble* BMH t73a
76 J.M. van Kempen, *Anniversary gift,
   given to Abraham Kuyper to mark the
   25th anniversary of De Standaard*
   SPKK m188
77 J.A. Kruseman, *Abraham des Amorie
   van der Hoeven* SPKK 516
78 Anthonius Brouwer, *The raising of
   Jaïrus' daughter* ABM s479
79 J. Verlaan *Religious service of a breakaway congregation in a Gelderland
   farmer's home* SPKK s18
80 F.W. Mengelberg, J.H. Brom, C. Lindsen, *Devotional cabinet with crucifix*
   ABM v489
81 O. Mengelberg, *Detail of a stained
   glass window* ABM v278g
82 J.H. Brom, *Chalice* BMH m10412a
83 Dutch?, *Gold brocade chasuble*
   ABM t2322a
84 Belgium, *Madonna wreathed in
   flowers* BMB v1a
85 J.Th. Toorop, *Girl at prayer* ABM
   te159
86 Joost van den Toorn, *St Hubert*
   RMCC b256
87 Dolf Henkes, *St Willibrord* RMCC
   s205
88 Ossip Zadkine, *Piëta* ABM m1934
89 Jacques Frenken, *Blue Madonna*
   RMCC b119
90 Reinoud van Vught, *Untitled* RMCC
   s250
91 Aziz Bekkaoui, *Habit* RMCC t244
92 Guido van der Werve, *Number Two
   (Just because I'm standing here
   doesn't mean I want to)* RMCC v889
93 Jeroen Offerman, *The Stairway at St.
   Paul's* RMCC v888
94 Ruudt Peters, *Liturgical plate* RMCC
   v887a-h

Colophon

This book has been published to accompany the permanent exhibition *History of Christianity in the Netherlands* on display in the Catharijneconvent Museum from September 2006.

Published by Waanders Uitgevers, Zwolle in association with Museum Catharijneconvent, Utrecht

Authors Saskia van Haaren, Babette Hellemans, Jeroen Koch, Tanja Kootte, Janneke Raaijmakers, Joost de Wal, Guus van den Hout (foreword)

Editorial committee Nicolette Bartelink, Saskia van Haaren, Guus van den Hout, Colin Huizing

Design Manifesta, Rotterdam

Photography Ruben de Heer, with the exception of frontispiece Studio Wil van Dusseldorp, p. 8 Jan Hoogsteyns and p. 92 Rik Klein Eggink Fotografie; ill. 88, 90 and 94 c/o Beeldrecht Amsterdam 2006

Pictures editor Kees van Schooten

Translation Niall Martin, Amsterdam

Printing Waanders Drukkers, Zwolle

Information on Waanders Publishers:
www.waanders.nl
Information on Museum Catharijneconvent can be found on
www.catharijneconvent.nl

ISBN 90 400 8223 5
ISBN/EAN 978 90 400 8223 8
NUR 694